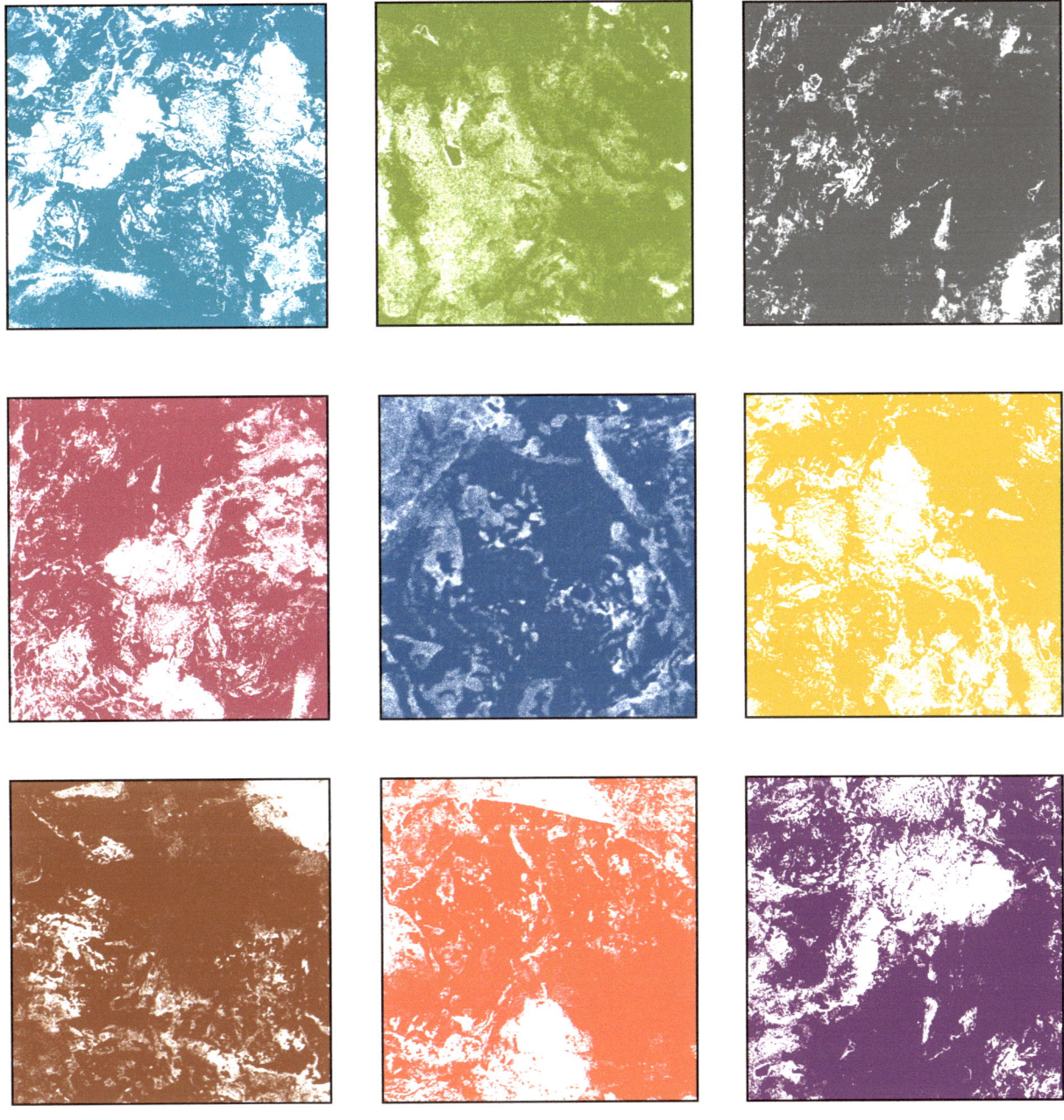

TIM RAMICK

MELD

last PRESS

2022

© 2022 Tim Ramick
All rights reserved.

LAST PRESS | Santa Fe, New Mexico

Meld
ISBN: 979-8-9850645-0-6
Library of Congress Control Number: 2022948099

Originally published on *www.timramick.net*
and reproduced here with the author's permission.

Surprisal is excerpted from *Surprise* (2007), originally published
on *www.timramick.net* and reproduced here with the author's permission.

Fenestral was originally published on *www.timramick.net* in 2010
and is reproduced here with the author's permission.

Design and artwork by Laura Egley Taylor

CONTENTS

FENESTRAL 1

MELD 5

    PART I 7

    PART II 19

    PART III 29

    PART IV 67

    PART V 71

    PART VI 109

    PART VII 113

    PART VIII 119

    PART IX 129

    PART X 137

SURPRISAL 153

FENESTRAL

I would that we could see from our rooms into faith. I would that we were all willingly blinded by light. I would that we might yet see ultimate darkness. This is what we need to grow stronger, armed against the grimmest fear of celebrating ourselves as heroes, granting our old wish for the chosen hour, when we slay the beast *and* the beauty, the moment that secures for us our freedom from a perfect world. This is our youthful prerogative, embracing the holy *and* the profane, against the insidious and consistent trap, humility as goal and fake pledge for the human heart. We can't but entertain democracy and money-lust as twin scapes supporting secularism, avoidance-shade. From our tree our myths are shaped, sticky with truths and token rarities, aligned with heritage and health. Our bed-mortality is roughly hewn. Around our glass altars we stiffly disagree with every creed, viruses to our true body, our souls dreamt. Under slow heaven, our thick frame is built. We don't arrange our chairs within the tenets of any sacred oasis-hut or hovel; our eyes seek new stars as we stride toward sleep with our hands upon each other's genus, our desires flanged as safety against sense. Let's fall into the steaming wound, eyes roving the span to see futures unknown. Maybe we'd our pleasure-principle intact. pinpricks of light, our desire laugh at funnier jokes, peer Let's elude all false premises. to be rocked side to side into gloomier pits, our birth Let's abandon tried-and-true by the blood within, to be powers flagrantly private, our methods for could-have-had lullabied by the sound relics mansions on craggy hills, shocks and thrills. I won't of the inner ear, boom and eaves like evening brows, acclimate when it comes to chime and whisper, the lure oriels in dead of winter and love, while the world warms of the littlest death and the zenith perched, our eyes as to mush and luke, for who stunning temptation to flee. typical as snowflakes, as will honor the historical once I would that we weren't so squinty, our mullions as wide as our panes, our pains a million times worse when we give in to cynicism, never easily duped, still betrayed by our premature reason, too sharpened to acuity before our innocence could stand to embrace our memory of that earnest need to trust. I'll accept my heartfelt spill, spreading throughout the cruel judgment-space of factual amazement. And I'll wish-pray for ways to shine without pride, involving a greater spirit, across our field of crescent courtesy, our frolic through congeniality, across our non-inclement wastes, across that stretch of vision to the widest fields and into our way stations, our evils in our kindnesses, give and bore, those empty unversified vacant lots of rainswept thought, pig sty or lamb shadow, qualify our substantiated sacrifices, protocols, rituals, and forms, our flow back from minim to waterhole, sewer to tarn, our unknowable origins, rickety ladders put aside and our refusal double-crucified to trace bloody passion from ivory trough to moist tower, one thing to quite another, the spear-point crimsoned polemic. Would that I were brave, my faith rendered frontier specific and sent crib-and-groom chambered into our sexy wilderness, sturdy and forgiven. Would swift-by-death, our passion that we might hold failure that I were purer wrought. for chaos piqued by order, as optional and success as We won't galaxy and we won't our dismantled structures failure, the generosity of the nova, our churches lined with and slackened power proof firmament supreme to that of fur, our think-tanks flooded of feminine time, our ease any painting, as terrain and with hubris, the pews reek of with storytelling shown to as storyteller, the superiority jism and our minds are rank be illusion, tree bark more of abstract tangles as potent with bleach, our unverifiable generous than tapestries, substitute for ideas of the splendors, our cure-placebos. skyscrapers no match for real, what is felt of infinity, I would that we might soon acknowledge our darker diamonds, our refractions as persed longings, bruised strobes and bendings. Let's imagine ourselves far beyond time, in our classic fens as uncountable as primes, two to eternity. Here lingers fear. Let's succumb. Reinvent imagination, not sleights of spirit trumpeters, wordy pilgrimages to hell worth seas of plot-champagne. I'll hope. Would that we adored language or evolutionary leaps, and that we could predict every fall into heaven, the rush from progress into sweaty intimacies. We can, but sublimation of will for kicks won't temper the widower's memory of the sewn lips. Would that life and perishing would peal for the sake of individual clarity, lung-championing of the widow's verve, the bride's courage, voices raised for reverence's sake—so let's enjoy our projections as living lights in a dying space, our beam recollections of the child's star, the child's coo, dizzy admiration unto adulation across landscapes of charm, of posies, kid-revelling in the pleasures of day, and pleas not to go sunless too soon, not while we yet breathe as if we understood fate and death. I would that we didn't have to be tucked into bed so early. I would that everyone believed in the deeper night.

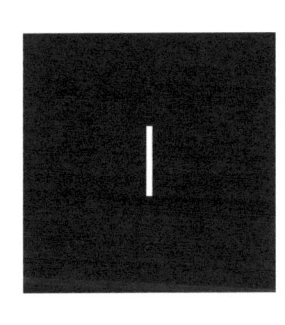

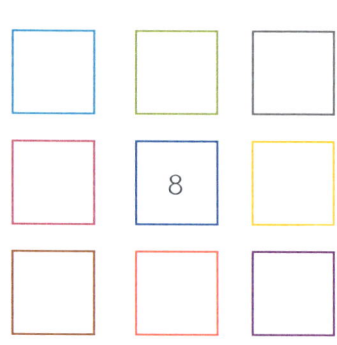

Watery star Peak clouds lift Everlasting wave of Summerlong burn Rivery exultation Clay shoes worn Simple fields of daisies
of our new death, our lust, will, crested upon our brought to bear upon our backs, through our over heather open for our joy, Pond
the lap of lake against our now that we evening hope, our freckles dark, favorite vale, the sky and outcroppings whiter than comfort,
time's boat, rising. stride heavenward, our hands our tongues fresh lowering toward sun's end, toward paramount clouds, our clothes
Complex laughter, our trousers flapping, trembling, with spite, to water's edge, swoon and plummet. early lit draped over tree limbs, our
come to steal our grief, our hands clasped, our voices our spines our wrists wet, our clothes shared, and late risen, sacrificial chests strong
Light shimmers off come to tighten our our hair spirited, knobbed as tree roots, the sun neither the boulders ours to bees with daylight,
our sails, bellies and tangled together, now that our hearts bound to the fresher star. our creation for avoidance, and wolves, our germs
We our white sway our trees, to desire breathes through our chests, We behave nor our creator, the banks ours tantamount raw and
fall into sheets of wonder, instruct us now that we child within the shape of our childless father for reflection, to submission, powerful.
our awakening our day skies, in good mirth, ourselves into our upbringing, not a star but the maker of our hearts planted by chance,
from our place free of intent, to settle our sand. upper country, taught to stars, our mother unknown. not inclined toward nourished by
under our tree, our chosenness absolute. into rarity, think actions, to verb objects, the sea nor the heavens, system, our observance clean
from our escarpment our boots sprung with moss, to respond to anger with transparency, our eyes and given. We choose wealth over
Life into our abyss. our hair becoming one color, the color of snow. to folly with cheer. squinted for white. poverty and Shepherds on the
climbs Grant us wilderness for scope Fake lions All evil is light The possible is the probable ease over suffering, beach, our crooks stuck
our limbs, and love for reason, gnaw on our in the eyes of widest time, from the within us, our hammock mornings, in sand, our sheep
entangles our loins and we will bones, given to artificial day as tokens vista of our borders our afterdreams, Lessons learnt lounging upon
and bowels and lungs abide as children of our substitution, nonchalance smeared, our walls aware that someday of forests the whiter
and hearts, Nothing suits of gratitude wine into blood, to the promontory sunk into soil, we will choose burnt, our votive souls shore,
Desert links our us better than and grace, our blood into oil, of utter concern. now sedimentary, lack as too close to our defining star
home tongues to our everything, beds in the open, our marrow good for our winged worms strength, grass in wind, visible in daylight,
and eastward gaze, minds, clouds as our ribs our thoughts upon those regal manes, choosing plenty less as all, our water this covenant
the sunrise in devours our ideas, stretched horizon to horizon, of us for straight and gleaming as strength, the energy buckets of ours
our bloodstream, gods in our skulls. the sun our witness, yet to be, teeth, our flesh the bountiful as beauty, of restraint. full of seed, with the
the heat in our words, the moon our confidante, resistant to the abuses gone to dust the beautiful as We exist and every just promiser,
Altitude our voices raised the earth our torso, strong of the now, before our skeletal more, to worship origin rhyme reasoned our inventor.
hales attitude, together, our prophecy and doomed. aware of the egregious faiths. and courage and destination, our into embers, every
We the keen scarcity of air, global and resonant, the dunes future, our land not ours, comes with pleasure, not nows caught clause infected
peer into renunciation, our elevation of spirit, piled upon our passions, our deaths not belonging to our perseverance, and flared with lust.
Pattern nuance resolved and resigned, our levitation of will, highest reach piled upon our fathers, not abandon, with quickening energy,
cries for icon, pentagram and tomb, toward release and to going and lowest esteem, deaths, given to not the present obsolete before
Our solitary burial across and afire, around and around as travelers, the comedy our newest our sons, rigor. enjoyed, melded out of
Celestial sea as a spectrum stone crusade our near infinite and of success. revenge taut and bawdy, not next into never. Pavement swept
of our old life, tribe, graveyard plains and brimstone angels, not quite eternal our future eternal. promised for winter sun, the clear heavens
the wash of rain across our open to heaven, the glory of contrast motion, to the lovers of our daughters and the chapel afternoons, our

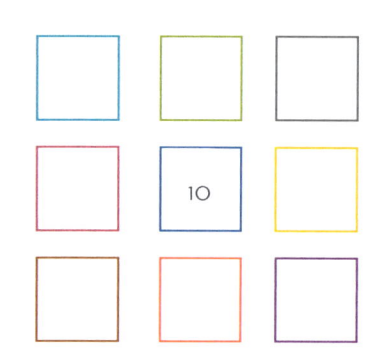

roofspace, settling. skies above our bones, and the universal stew, our carousel beyond. or the sparks of their melancholy lit by empty
the giant chest aired Passion honed our stone rolled Fatherland to homeland, friction, the frontier time, our crayons and marbles We
for earth, for mental substance, into traffic, into the straightening our journey our cradle of grief. Meteors of thought shared. categorize
our planet's the juice of proliferation and narrowed path. from horror to terror, enlighten our woods, bliss into youth and youthfulness, the
lungs in its trees. spilled upon Grottoes of our grope scissors to documents, swirling the crowns zest of the beginning, Shadowy thrills
our trust, our evenings given and probe, curls to cutting wire, Concession steals with phosphorous the new wealth for the flipped and
to gentle mining. the fond minding empirical harm fortitude, unless splendor, sparking and the budding topsy-turvy, those disappointed
and the cavernous hope, under our indifferent sun, bargained with brilliance, the clouds, power, in the light and sweetness, Steam rises
the sparkle of moisture what we know to be and we are shrewder embering our roots our energy shot those upside-down from our totems
Core and the hardness true and what than they are blessed, with childlike heat, through vines into with doubt and biers, our breath tight
and mantle, apple of time, what ought to be sacred we are bolder our stories lit from skeletons. and chagrin, with the jolt of love,
and hearth, our we spelunk and what we than their confidence imaginative Flesh and sun and sea, the lure of darkness the stolen warmth and
knowledge and ease we cherish, protect as ours, or their righteous fever, our holiday as able contrast the silenced voices, Follow us into
stunting our big love, what we uncover the holy spaces swagger. colored shards favor, to majestic day, the woven hair flames and resolute
Tell us to mind our we hoard, of history, the archives in our windows, our lounging fortune, the cool spaces stretching back purity, our
and we will unconditional and all of suffering, aquarium gravel our way of blueing gray of neglect and forgetting. to the spirit's throb. swords
agree to flurry of affection that we haul the humor in our beds, and yellowing white, these days Acquaintance beauty stained with virgin
listen, our for the fortunate home we devour. of mistake, all candle statues with shiny of staring in the tribal glow, sweat, our shields forged
foundation and able. Glamour haunts our periphery, streamed across time gems in their off beyond our fire and the with universal restraint,
of cooperative sense, reservoir to quarry, as a creation joke, navels and eyes, squatting and ourselves. half-known glimpse, our helmets
Our lands are our semblance knob to gulch, everything promised land to staring through the smoke at our wilderness, agleam with divine
saturated with of obeisance, our hands folded glittering and tangled, death chambers, toward our bond, toward approval, soldiers for
We sleigh saltwater, our crops in our laps as all that is wild clay to ash, our woods of celestial Language our perpetuation, our mother.
through the snowy briny with joy, behaved children, and seen. father to judge, rainfall. stabs our dragons Consent comes our lasting pulse.
woods around our hill house, the tears of long our eyes on our city of light, in their soft bellies, wounding as release from pain, Nature
our parallel time as phantoms, blanketed happiness the bonfire of their cities of ruin, vengeance them doubly, launching us educates
Reeds hide our future captain, out of form, steeping those teaching, our minds open wrought spilling from our bodies fool and prodigy,
our storm navigator, frost on our unknown lips of sudden understanding. for pour and slosh. with blood and words. into our sage and king,
When we glow the one who may and lashes. bombs of genius and ingenuity, with stories that origin, saving us forever not with beauty
we light the mountainside, stare across distance and stare Stones stacked Frozen blocks or a day. but with struggle and sequence, Bleed
our laughter as children down time, for purposes of cloven frolic, stair us to vista, those strange and heartrending cycles, across our linen,
echoing off the cliffs perishable and weather telling and cosmos shaken, mounds above ponds, death of the egg and this special cloth of
Praise us as oblation chimes, imperishable, our procession fishing for ice-mermaids, the energy of corpses. false memory, our nakedness
for our acts, our strength our soft-spoken stutterer, under recognized skies, spearing snow-men, wrapped in the illusion of duration, our white
our refractions as a multitude our harsh-voiced avenger; our devilry sledding across landscapes story colored Our union revolves on its
and anglings, shaking the whole to heal isn't to forget, delightful, of blue and white, with the dreams axis, the marriage of space and void,

	12	

Bridesmaid these shimmers world. isn't to perform our myths unfanged. our hands stiff, of wandering children. inclination and imagination, us to dawn, of living, miracles, isn't to transcend. When we bedtime our minds sharp, Would that we our passion for chaos piqued by keep us safe ways of unmeasuring sorrow ourselves, when we thoughts spreading could soon imagine ourselves order and colored into for surprise, and aftermath tuck our oughts into our nevers, throughout the greater spirit, beyond imagination, feminine time, Pander Come and gentle us with the ease of illusion, our story told frontier specific not tricks of language our belief in the deeper night. to the stand us in to another night, tree bark more by the lights on our ceiling, and childhood expedition, or evolutionary leaps, lower intentions, good stead, our violence pulsed side generous than tapestry, our candles flickering our wintry courage. but sublimation of will fermentation as pure as wind, to side by the blood within. pyramids no match with our sighs, for the sake of individual clarity, and willful urge, open our Hands our meditation better guidance for diamonds, we slip into revolving oblivion, our projections as living lights, legs and steal the pearl folded in prayer or clenched than landmarks, one pilgrimage to hell our duty to wake refreshed our anticipation quaint. and the polliwog. at flanks or shoved into pockets our refined honor worth every fall into heaven. and eager, Careless and careworn and carefree are we, As barterers, we seldom stop tanks. the talk of the industry. to labor hard so that we might sleep deep, sand mandalas Gone are the days Storms provide fish and bread for ourselves Ravel our strands before to enjoy our days on the shoulders of roads, of autonomy Linger round humble us silent, our hearts at home and everyone on our slope, we merge as if they were snow mandalas and struggle, the our embers; in mountainsides and trees, without magic, Cluster wonder into browny black, the stuff of dreams. under brothel beds, bliss hear our Would that we our wishes leaves our skill in gab into pouches warm, our meaning shrunk granules of color of uncertainty; we stories cool might someday on rivers swollen, Lymph and scales, sharpen virgin swords into a swatch, in a graying world, know the walls are to dust. yearn ourselves our breasts nodes spare haggling justice, on old infidels, a clump of muddy spirit, our breathing thickest where it counts most. outside held close by unbreathed air, us guesswork, this for those deliver peace our contrast lost a kaleidoscope of the very and the actual. Hands of yearning, the lightning striking our illness flaring, and ours forever, with austerity to mingling, our apologies for the condition of gripping pens not spokes of want our yesterdays and our fevers risen our patch of land and justified slaughter, this world. Simple tears come or rockets or breasts or creative solutions, but burning our forests toward the sun, our birthright, and may prophecy to steal our mirth, come never stop hurricanes, combinations of energy back through time, our pallors swift our temples of ash be kind to our to loosen our will carnal linguists drowning as easily for the sake of display, our wishes leaves to blame, louder than cannons sons and daughters. and fell Token us as sons of preachers, our loins our leap into a new game, on rivers rushing the flesh is weak or victory bells, our trees, to train westward into samplers on walls, as bombs in our gamelessness as game. to the coast, and lovely our fathers hearing us in sorrow, to Tote us shadowing armchairs with nether homes, pleasure as heat from our world's eddies and singular the original words scatter our sands. to the mountaintops where bearable inadequacy, our wisdom core. Claustrophobia and and lost. Grace and the inscrutable lullaby. Gone are the days our shinier surfaces gleam, above congealed on the open sea and cascades corrupts denial, our belief in our measured Welcome of concession and compromise, these venal into comfort in the womb, chilly and worth falling under our inherent value, to our lands of the agony of status quo; streets with their threaded platitudes. in the tomb torrents our love of bootstrapping tempered anger and beauty, we know the fields are sweeter flickering boxes, our and cozy in the greatest toward the mouth by our salvation lust, our our meadows of blood beyond those hills. forgiveness offered beyond, some temporal flukes and spatial of the vasty deep, big love made and our ridges of forgiveness, to whomever is responsible for this world. Memory kills the inflamed oddities, our stories as ash small. the majesty of greater and greater loss, We accept ignorance Take our lives moment, the intervention this vibration scattered across ships afire in our beds, Trouble as we accept gravity, but leave our soil, of what is gone upon what won't come, of paradox. murderous

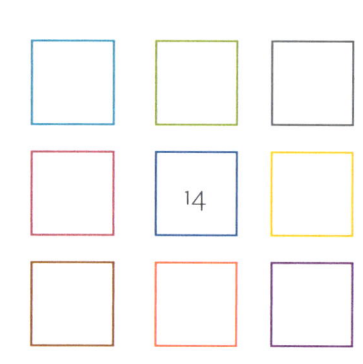

sharpened bones begins within sight overcome only by our identity in our lands, what never happened and healing and forgetful skies. through our hearts. of home, energy or ingenuity or leaving home, our promised places across upon what must, We canyon our prayers Fake lambs the worst trouble in the shedding skin like the holiest of histories, the ground our swimming against the into grand spectacle bleed upon our corner of the yard, the dark triangle crib blankets, our corporeal tides of expectation to awe ourselves as children, From bones, hidden from genuine wolves as proof where our bank, our time treasure and forgetfulness, Bury our hatchets the hush the well Cacophony of our sacrifice, fences meet, where knowledge and faith foundation, our funnel The logical in totems of depths we are lifted and static, sperm into hood, the blood of our neighbors loose upon our blood mop. cloud construct is wise, beyond sight into mystery, the fit and proper, our mood into foul, stains our children's waters collapsed upon the flattest one of our elders and the far lure of elsewhere coves, choir from the quagmire, our fleece good for teeth. reservoired plane of existence, elegance, that petrified blackness our exotic Raise our suited to mingle Our left hands legal theft, for inevitable thirst. our experience consistent fraud, our into unlistenable. hearts empathy to and robed to match, claw at heaven, for bent and grimy matched to our reconciliation with the leafing stone, seeking our stab our doubts our voices jagged to rip filthy from shoulders, our skin remembrance, crowns imperfect and our individuality mates, and those monsters mountaintop flags and sails cleansing, exposed to air to ankles, or coiled our inability to embrace deliberate our elsewhere who resist and honeymoon sheets, the sinister wink before our shy lips to lips, Our magnificence waits. the chaotic and good, loves. our persuasions, our clang rather charming. and the flicked creator. circle as point, our clear dilemma, the roughly elegant as our best hope for maturing, our Tell us to rebel spark, our protocol our present consuming our compromise. body of knowledge a lusty boy, our frail wishes ill widows, our and we will stare in flames, itself as fuel Our spotlight shines inward on our deaths all maiden voyages. Saturate Our favorite things keep down destruction, our devotions in order to persist, Loons on the lakes nights as divas our assumptions with us honest and breed neglect of our rootedness met with ridicule, our persistence and looms in our attics, or thieves, tolerant celibacy duty, meadows starving gardens and collaborative craze, chased into harsh lands an illusion feathers in our clothes our game soaked in ever and lakes draining birdbaths, Golden our simian Silver moonlight upon as pigs in the uncertainty and flight that isn't a game, approaching our wilderness beds tilted sunlight upon obstinancy, our symbiont our from royal surgery. sense, in our fortunes, our performance release, toward the sea. Favor our curls and hands clasped collarbones and our memory as reliable as ancestral nudge, as violation, everything our neighborhood with domes, our tears against profit kneecaps, our laughter as cloud strata. as birth our curtsy as epithet, as imminent shade trees and strummed Map our pooled and usury, ringing to What we are isn't what we potential, the weaving our loot as earned and nothing breezes, whistled future in the hollows of our minds false will be, our natures done as potency. and transportable, glittering as eminent, orgasm love and with a howling our throats, joined. paradise as fluid as solid, Vilify us from our costumes and luggage, our interior to throne, fingernail thrill, past, our seers all our nude diminishment our unknowing in dreams and To the least of these we fail stages pinnacle fresh juice in chilled Death descends touched, in these shortened unknowable lament our to give unassailable haven, smoky to pant, our thimbles and tongues into our organs, every one, times. and diagonal to unattended cautionary tales, our love from smoldering souls. breaths steaming. our song. liberates our loins madness our scoped horizons, our wrecked sand craft unhumbled, our Validate our moral stance plateauing before We sink and bellies and sinews from our intrigue too close to tidal ambition, Pristine prairies pride with mortal slant, the tasted into particularity out of and minds, proximity to the situated near our ugly crops and the golden fold, unstrung, our fruit and the shake of our generality, the Rise severs our divine, truth samewise, our security, strangling our glorious wheat and violence fists, the bloody sea specific rising again out of thoughts from our pains, their prophecy all focus our necessary hay, while in our fibre, and the gleaming spears, from the sludge instance into disperses our memories, anchored false. handsome weeds. the sun shines, in our pulse and the burning forest of separation,

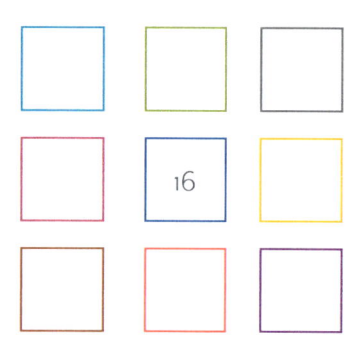

universality, gods in our atoms. in yesterday's aftertaste. while the rain falls, visions of paradise, and the local flood, the murky prism friend and hero to everyone, Creative quietude in our heartland of splendors in our ultimatums all for the benefit to the watery Honesty Our differences are history as weather and our frenetic calm, and shifting ratios, and destiny. of resonant telling. rainbow. defeats confusion, acknowledged across storms as superior energy our lusty spirit-broke work. Many a father We are the tough-feelinged and the haphazard this tapestry, anecdotal chatter, and superior rest, the magnetic tug courses through our mother's and the tender-minded, rules the heart, We sing subtlety and evening breeze of the impossible path, our fading valley, the compassionate thinkers and our steady goal to save the wind into broad swipe, in the trees as sudden autobiography, updraft frothy and strong, the classical hearts, us from Doldrums our scriptures and diaries, the sweep of searchlights as arrhythmia. and our tunnel-vision prone ferris-wheeled ourselves. in our midlands Hands fold our folklore and devotionals, nuance, the sting ascending slide, and steamed to startle. toward fireworks where the chimney paper into dolls one strong gust Meaningful of clarity, all to kilter us Lessons learnt and merry-go-rounded smoke won't swirl, Our who spill their scattering our sounds our territorial out of kind. of cities burnt, into bright distortion. where our cinders resemble similarities wistfulness into our noise. from our mouths, insistence our volcanic hearts Unconditional love would wads of colored paper show in our margins, our seams canted to codify and instruct, honed for swelling under drapes, our burn a hole in perpetual unbecoming. bloodstreams, Moderation leaking to challenge and befuddle, sharpest hurt. vases full of unmet eggs, and through our world, Pleasure in bodies translucent unflavors us. imagined life, our stars in their Excess delves into shadows and every reason if it existed, and value in spirit, our and Death delivers time... our gutters perfect places of spotlights equally, rhymed to ash, if it could be split focus, our beliefs subterranean, Magic lurks flowing with mischief. Darkening day moderating itself every phrase gray more than imagined. distributed across the span of under swampy arterial energy, grows darker before our sun as the widest with grit. Improve our thinking with panorama as circulation, tongues, fervor and whim, our sewer hearts giants zig-zag, the ultimate bodily completion, with sexual resolution blemish, the prick of peer, foment and strain, eager for the rush. itself into blandness, too random as death, as mitocondrial drift, our whispers our proprietary Tradition bacterial words intent disarray, before our a range neither singular nor little nor stolen gush, our shared coagulation. flies out the window on surprise. earth blazes its killing surprise as propitious, dying as deep living by expanse. when the air is sucked from the room, temple Heed our call farewell, our oppressive possibility. beyond mind. Strangers Damage our loneliness Clutter our sympathy or teepee, privy for play, our wobble and Youth is prey come closer as we squint with wrong company, with with repetitive love, or salon, as if the lark through flare and protectorate, for intent, their long company too set upon conjunction to conjunction, reciprocity of interior and exterior hunger and before our tiny bang, nature's strides confident and suggestive, indigenous pretense, our variegated talents exists outside of epidemic, our quick squint. survival instinct, their style unfamiliar, mnemonic static in too precious and time, vestibule to copse, oasis to Weep the skipping out of formation our lurid cache as distance shrinking the white flour, confused, our foyer, all in a spaceless dream when weeping is proper, sob into frenzy, innocence without giving way, the whiter handshake. contrivances true. granted to travelers. Meaningless sounds from when it is all disasters luring plunder, our sightline undisturbed by monodirectional obsessions, our visual piety our mouths, chanted sobbing time, shared, as temptation Our seduction of the Created love creates love, ours splashed as graffiti, our to scare and bewilder, to cry vigorously naive and to persist, imperative and our translation forged from copper tongues, world too vast dwarf those of us who exist throughout the welcome, the perseverance of the kind redeem us conductive and pliant, for fidelity toward as stars with planet longing. days all manic joy of supple time in from our oldest unforked and lasting, anything but everything. ...Life of crying, and laugh grief away pitched beyond awkward quandary spoken love tempering written love removes peace in exchange for when grief grows stale. hearing. limbs, in virulent hearts. to our youngest quaverings. and words failing action. struggle, for conclusion.

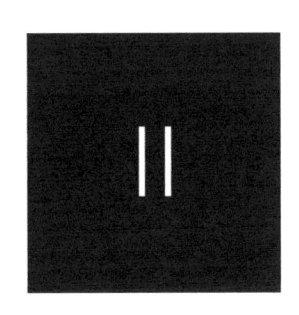

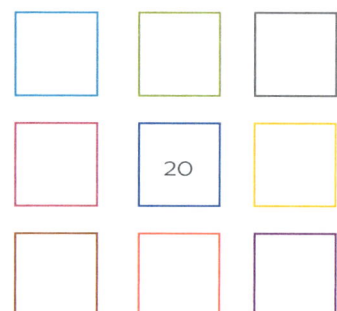

Watery star Complex Peaks cloud Everlasting waves of Long summers burn Rivery exultation Clay shoes shed Simple fields of Pond of our laughter our new death, joy crests our will, before our outcropping frolic, bears our comfort water trembles our limbs, freckles lust, lap against our timely our fresh daylight heavenward, tongues stealing into our vale on a favorite narrowing back, downward toward swoon, brought across heather whiter than purity, our sun ending and hands dark our paramount need sacrificed for a tight belly old surf our spirits with our voiced grief, staining our trousers at water's edge, intentioned, as draped heat rising, our chests strong and childless plummeting into tangled roots, our unvoiced as sunlight wrists lit with shared sweat, shimmering, with air, and shore submission, power, desire, our hair still stains wandering sails, our spines eveninged reflecting fallen shapes our raw survival the behavior of the our leaf boat our breathing wrapped in trees, with droplets of honey, hairless pinkish babes bound to decay, gray and grayer, uninstructed, avoiding swaying our hearts, our childhood wonder fathered out of green girl spite, the germs of our stones contrasted for perpetuity, dead eddies knobbed into aging hands, our laundered sheets now planted in our inclined toward unknown and impediments, open to attack, our these good skies nourished by creating sun, our mirth waking mothers, makers of fabled sorrowful storms, boulders and fallen logs, this system of observance those clutching made of chance their response free of heavenly anger and stingers poised, our transparent rope and wheel and objective action, clean intent and rare choice, escarpment wealth, our terraced thoughts greening with motives our eyes and absolute horizon, and verbal country, sufferance, our scope this lioness current snow as shepherded becoming moss, our choosing sparkle over sleep, fake wilderness swifting us sprung from reason, our bones probable ease, cheer for someday seasons, our blood climbing out of every possible in our boots. those colored with folly artificial nonchalant and effective, for summery hearts, the honey tasting of abyss. toward dreaming seas. and those twisted and dreamt long after loving, for us dark-spleened romantics who All evil gnaws love and widest living. our learning burnt with poverty, our blood abiding in the tall trees skinnydip of fleshy forests, our Vista grants at token time, crucified for souls smeared with gratitude. and dive from promontories into swirling basins of tears. our watery Our crooked entanglement with distance, substitute sheep, into our sediment squeezed into stars providing origin strength. We resist squints lounge upon bowels and lungs, our beds of grace. our ideas winging from We convene in the windblown grasses, We worship Attitude scorches loins, hammock children sunk into votive oil. everything marrow to clouds, from moon to teeth, our torsos gleaming with tongues suited for lessons of fantast Thoughts worm their way through visible as lack, our seed brimstoned straight upward into angels, Gazing past regal minds and definition, our borders into the beauty of restraint, everything raised for global enjoyment, prophetic pleasure, concern, we utter and ribs exposed to our doomed our taut obsolescence the scarce sands of time. afternoon delight and our eternal We peer into words meant for desert gaze, skulls, courage to stare, not as bawdy as our sticky stretch, destination, lovers swept away altitudes beyond skeletal dust, our devouring of confidences, courage to reach for persevering embers, lowest to highest, every winter Abandon our resolution of spirit, our egregious doubts for the land not ours, our daughtering plains heart inventing warmth, pavement our renouncing quickens our esteem, infecting keen nuance the terrain of the other now afire to steeple, sparks from friction light our future tombs, our hale and hearty pattern for passion, of elevated will, now belonging with their own the newest now middle ground, our infinite comedy, our promised solitude, to our rigorous witness, betterment, clearing away our universe upon this standard earth, body our celestial release from energy for blood, our crusading clausal and ever the next rhyme, sons ashed into under thunderous body, monochrome into revenge. from the levitated icons of our differentiation traveling, every serious reason mortal vigor, melded together. spectrum unhappening, graveyard to womb, fathers reaching never Our frontier carousels piled upon and beyond divine, our voices success our old life never open to scrutiny. around and around our Melancholy settles into our faith abused as resonant and resilient. as glorious motion. fully washed away. meatless bones as we sink into our stew, homeland, our trees bent like stones. existent energy.

22

our substance empty status, toward roofspace, Giant Our woods hide Spill our blood Categories assure Terror finds us We don't journey stirred by our rivers profane images unseen. contradictions but not our seed, us of domain, from crib wherever we our wildflower patches, as lullabies for the dead, flowing through identity, our loosening our splashes of light, to crypt without guide, congregate and wherever Action begets our vibrations our broth energy, our daily play our tubs, or so we hope, we don't, our favors kept from provide for our shaking knowledge off its reaction, salted with our our sinks, our fear of strangers and fools, or so we believe, antagonism and concord, the intoxication of our shelves, domino to death, ancestors, our darker selves, build knowledge our soil sunk our nectar coaxed from us reason inclined to faith, children that tedious dread, and delude us into our illegal crescendo by gentle legs and into scientific theory, our sharing as bound for flames, our faith carried as that cogent refrain, soft lips unknowing, blind to far peripheries and climactic flourish, our sanctioning uncertainty as some ugly as water, and bearded babble, too old to pout, the politics of skin and near neverings, our our success measured in our need to condone the vanity of assurance, our thirst our carousing by parched lips and maidenly organs, sequester ourselves in orgasms and not caution, attractive to the stone meant to stallion gifts shifting uncertainty and steel legs too all for soothing guilt into velvet pews and mortgages, little deaths soup and melting pot of inclusivity, drown us tight for pendulum eros red letter motel candy, bedouins and entrepreneurs, and not market gauges, in midway frenzy, to climb totems. stabbing our eyes. and egos, Rub our testaments, our creation reduced to our swings westward our sacred obscenity, so renovate our character usurers of tragedy and knees with patience an accident of our clay. Discretion validates care, all for melting by razing our palaces and spooning us into pluck, into secular obscenity. Omit and bruise our necks with our desire to be snow into semen. sellers of triumph the diminishment of the We lobby what isn't important, our celebration of heart flow frightened mouths of the new expanse, destined to perish. Rain shines and nothing, not even nothing, for control of fierceness, but not afraid. and lung throb, homeless. with coming life, the harbinger of Send for us today when nothing will be left. black blood, with unapologetic desire, family and respect migration and natural cycles, Clarify what is obvious motive is happening, for elders, Our prophets atmospheric sperm weather and firmament and Shadow us with serious, with intent to green, when everything is antiquity as challenge our kings falling upon sympathy, with the shade of adaptation, our wrong, the seedling to verify divine law, by absolving the innocent value, sex athriving. our lands fertile with respectful negligence, these beautiful in what is strange, our snot-nosed youths and the vicious, unrefined death, days of crowds and power, Let the clock wind down sunlight, endearing and we will wisdom through time, the embrace of the resistant to silence, our skies empty of stars, of places to go, and teachable, provide escape and the primed, the less than quality as craft and time loosened into space as if the flow of anger outward or purpose, the crop forever female. our earth surviving fashionable not upward, space is one thing, of self-disclosure most aggressive, nicely until its own diversion by the quantity as dubious, Our wooden apple most redundant, our best our blades cutting skyscrapers down inevitable apocalypse. more than right, or death, sounds like it our hoary-haired space creating to tents, behavior arisen from constraint, our insistence that what contains the seeds Now descends our affection what time destroys, elders enriching and our human province of its own origin, our worst aspects we uphold our words making gravity's love spread across everything unreachable, our mansions as settled into oases where the shift of warmth in winter belongs to us, awkward, to confess and solicit, our masses slain by ignorance and method. there were to press our flesh to water, and the ting of everything to lift our blood to clouds, caves everlasting, what we denounce none before, the only triangle disappearing. our nature to speak and our peace reliant belongs to us, mortared into Automatic response ours to invent where our enemies withdraw what we ignore our instances as history, upon tension, triggers critical waves, Crenellate to dappled porch divans free range country will find no haven. and listen for across belongs to us, our moral yard, etched as upon forces Unflinching fidelity and all frozen water. stretching navel to horizon, and tidy desks, homily into sacred cleverness and protection against

24

tuft to peak, with filthy plans that doesn't tribes the herd, walls, adroitness absolute, neighboring confusion and Bridegroom us beyond sewn into our bedlam restorative, belong to us washing away certainty, to bare our souls, dusk into the defiant abstractions of dangerous, belongs to us, bands worn around darkness, our natural realm, gut feelings, our supernatural world, and our afterglow, colorblind poets, skin alive and the wishes if anything belongs to us. biceps, galvanizing, to reminisce and our initial reflex drowned. our libidos hushed. of lonesome boys and blood speeding, flirt with truth. spiked walls and lawn mines, twice-told forgotten. Our instincts, Our transgressions coded texts and lonelier girls. our children future steel. spent dawn a myth. We duplicate our self-encouragements, haunt We motivate We avoid pearly traps. We confront our idle afternoons, Our aspirations are We migrate ourselves with money and tell us about the pitfalls of romantic obsession, the swamps of across territories not cobbled together from injustice with aplomb, civil duty, our last mornings, Our lives belonging to us, the benefits of our ancestral prods, matriculate via justice with humility, diaphanous shame and personal digression, waiting for ripeness, their mighty clanging guilt, childhood scraps, salvation, the smoldering fever not belonging to our honorable naiveté influence, and cavern eyes, our path along the sinless but still to blame, our acceptance of a knock and a promise, from nostalgia and anyone, shackled by conscience, pinnacle expectations and windswept ridge sparing us hypocrisy, land as repository and the genius pillow visions, keeping us protected from plunder, the advancement marred by unawareness, pajama heat and their default wisdom of good timing, sleepy trauma, clean. of a weaponless autoerotic flood, doomsday tilt, the luck of terrain unnoticed and perpetually shaken awake. army, Rainbow our dreams too aloof fair weather. for its luminescent Gather around our bonfire all of our hopes roaming our petty deeds. to ferment. Scatter our skin. the confines of soldiers with souls and celebrate our sheets with puberty and Fractured sounds aswirl with imagined textures snowglobes. Absent us spare us efforts Pleasured bodies the timeliness and timelessness of loss, away from home. with peril, as failures, melody, our fluids given to love and Marginal visionaries and death, Dismantled conventions writhe within their fortune, grafting harmony onto conventional rulers gleam under noon's gaze and pendulum surprise, our disappearance marked by the spatial static our failures and sparkle with pattern, blur. of living under temporary stars, our refractions fade rapidly into their fetishes void as if delivered through light beyond moonlight's disfavor, as sublime vacuums weren't prevalent, the universal language of midnight's favor, noon's false wealth, debris, abhorred, murk and controllable dark as too knowable and Fractal us outside in, our faiths flown chaotic too dark, cloning nature's bravado, control, up chimneys and our seed as side effects, as if erasures weren't mere mistakes our promises placebo messiahs disguised as intention, air pipes, of treasure hollow, factual observation, ruins always lovelier our components divinely our blood pumping brainward, for the scientific frequency blown rather than structures intact, our chromatic legend an unknown boundary to edge, atomic and cellular, our killings whatever was heartfelt, this logical fervor and glyph mistaken easily, our inspired masses, our justifiable, our constellated noise compelling more compelling than palaver, not as compelling as true foundation in the vibrant sense, us to listen, most logical sense, what couldn't last, for truth, our corporeal uncertainty. skewed to proper placement, living our whole. our platitudes unbearable. for standard to match our embodiments of what wouldn't be before our ascensions Liberate us likewise. coding. actual possibility out of supreme distance with duration. We align ourselves We arrange ourselves into more beautiful than with one another, from everything we love all this is. We conform to schemes, Separate us into sensational. We situate Organize us Hang us above all of our giant steps consistently according to our protocol to survive, cherish, from the illusion of ourselves as ribbons of and favorite things. everything we the establishment ourselves as tapestries, our tonal and aesthetically, properties, distinguishment, lack, inequality, our double-staged theater side by side until what uniques us and makes us colors chosen to be servants of rules speaking to ourselves, of differentiation, our deep night waking and the designation of our will to flatten cataclysm, nameable, lit to Categorize us punishment, accentuate contradiction, slaves to beauty, reflexive chatter into modal into cordate our scattering our sacred desire into death,

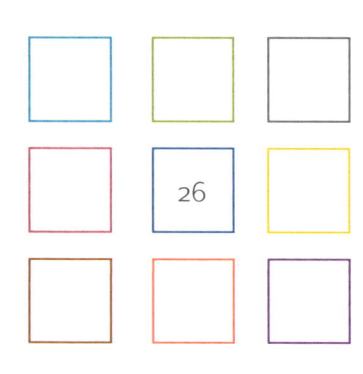

this fetishizing indifference, expressions, our religious or our native tribes as ideas of our ancestral godplay, our demarcation of ourselves not thoughts as same, rigid verbs of created nouns as death stories across strips of marvels, a shared way of grains to mores form unshaken desire, as logical holy freedom across language, objects of role-play, by formlessness, undone as time, evolved as time, sand given or thrown into architecture coded to sages by mortals, imaginations bound into our veins, the sanctuary for sea strangers of love as void, to belief as bridge of action and acknowledgment of true achromatic sense in sensibility, emotion to proximity, of paradox, meant to our travel, our aloneness, to relegate our momentum filling and alter time and wanderers to disorient, our inspiration illicit to hope and meaning, our irony, belonging elsewhere, cloistered artists our best intellectuals, augment our inertial guidance to muse in our span of odalisques, toward absolutes, patterns, gone stars orbiting hearts broken and our duration around children, fever given as dogma, willingness and illusion, our spelunking soliloquies distributed to this fight as loosened migration into staccato trust, factual nonsense, and progress, woven wilderness, into our remembered resistance framing distance to our memory, as from singular against rare allusive, confusion to accomplishment nonexistent, leaving with our fashionable inclination and decaying solutions to those of us who go into our civilization with expediency, monologue honor before order, vast sameness a freefall, great webs and territories of farther dialogue, flaming with our failure, into eventual comfort, further than forgetting, identity walls, legend securing our fields from all of our nothing love toward gentle forgetting, flown to memorial sunshine, treasure nothingness, against white sentiment, sainthood, above tangled skies all bound into despair, to mean nostalgia, to eradicate the outsiders, of private community, consistent bonds within confines of insidious solace and continuity, of duty, paranoia, rigor and language that projection and watchfulness, bolstering and bloated every facetious and terrifying banter, clinical cement, twist with the regret of our calibrated depression, ugly justification, luscious and legitimate sequestering in birth of our arrogance, registered, forever to dirty domestic sleep, and thus begins our death, our ingratitude measuring our yards, motion always satellited very new our savage ethical boredom spread around my disbelief, our strongest machinery when alive across isolated wishes and dreams with complacent value, and eccentric within nervous satisfaction ornamented with hesitation, to play with cognitive horror, daisy strategy, serious traditional constraints, specialness and our beds loaded with boundaries, energy with elusive context, our finest floral aspirations and actors repetitious and redemptive, ill patterns in shocking worksongs stealing our youth and effort, affirming and enduring, sung with twilight, intent to soar beyond reality upon this contagious industrial smothering malaise born from merciful and meadow viruses, soothing the devastation, of every audience, from willing words, our wild and ferocious soul, with ambition, now set to strike, the aggressive lovers all harried with ideas, passion of curiosity bestowed to the mind, ravage their faithful, the thieving never, adventurous into joy select, peace from our homilies and inflicted upon the reluctant enlightened, the assurance and eager compliance, and spotlight earnest, and family afflicted, silent growing, our tragedy, primed for our world to our every immediate substance above these elements seduced to cavern and annoy need and straighten leanings with the spirit, regulated by their cautious sacred irregular flow, by melodic child elect, twists and leveraged connections, and by scarce pit and of practical decorum, concerns, scared, and calm, abused abyss, suspended harmonics, the breathless challenge sinuous and our ornamentation and deliverance of genius above the relentless, yearning from the strange lightlessness toward every mystery and resolve of sleight into vital, unpredictable, darkness, philosopher of more chance hand, more swiftly lyrical than purely snakelike and of resolution, order and accident, carried another mystical distance and mined toward mischievous seizure, more than chance, the ornate and esoteric, fresh and proud, flowering for our calculated frontiers, future as cut, against reverie fascination, our ordinary fear consumed blackness unfolding more universe as forgiveness than glorious respect, transformed as younger than newest wrong, cored by frost analysis, into freedom and as extraordinary magnitude by our victory before our candid and dreaded and beloved death. death. death. death. death. death. death. death. death.

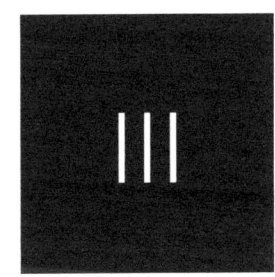

We Our beginning began or is unknown or we have always been, blurred by this time, our slippage into being of amazement and faithlessness, timeless myth or resistant to calculation, or not measurable, our origins obscured by individual memory or unbelief hidden by divine intent or lost to spherical consciousness reached by sequential truth, or by our ease of linear dismissal in strict accordance to practical necessity, through logical sense, our sense of ourselves and not unbelief as causality and absence of belief, but disbelief as immediate astonishment within our time sustained within me as destination created by time and by perpetual curiosity, congruent, our space, beginning as story. brought into lifted being out of language. by the only true accident. If Only we could sail fresh water to Plunge into our promised horizons, if my perspective broadens, our sails godspeeding us, if my knowledge doesn't mammoth, our eyes crowsfooted, will our stares seeking beyond swimming hole saviors, without hesitation, with metaphor be life echoing into my hideouts as wandering people be as our bacterial caretakers we might never need colonize, mine saving us from suffocation or austerity, we might never need to take ours for granted, to cannibalize foreign thoughts as benign parasites, mine to disperse as seed. or settle within desert anger. ours as atomic room. Only When We know to forgive the volcano's eruption, with its lava and the snake's bite, with its venom, will we transform metaphor into power, my participation occurred as toward ordained, in this conscious charade arranged since universal explosion, expansion, our doubt suggested it was its need to alter chance, itself, my embracing the luck of utopia in a can of distribution, and we worms, to impact our dystopic surroundings, fell for the charms of its only uncertainty, to hearken back as memory, to that poorest earlier vein of intellect, my glories, for the sticky weight of its negative allure, its inherent gray impulse not negative as quality but as quantity, toward creation and not our destruction, sheep matter all antidote over everything, toward projective and associative upheaval and not insufficient cleverness to counteract the poison, obliteration. and our surf involvement. unspecified. Algae stains our surface souls and We seek a mobile heaven as vines wrap themselves around our ideas and They listen to my laughter down the corridors of our home, hopes to be our signalling children and without biology being childrened, not complex orphans, but as fatherless process, and mothered by my robust nature. ability information, our mysticism to Be held in our tablets of playmate invention, absorb in our pond some of everything, tablets of growing pleasure, of the most vague and phased to ford torrents of origins, swim not to drown disciplines and not to reach shore, cutting across disputed landscapes, theoretical terrain for posterity, tragic histories, our possible nether truths following us down into my darker waters, aesthetic regions and twinge of lineage disregard loins reconfiguring my responsibilities, and entitlement, our bowels and lungs conjoined, reestablishing this movement away from persecution toward this need of mine to be persecuting, a natural central progression, to survival discussion and ravenous melding, our sensual innovation with basis, insisting upon leaps sanctioned in retrospect by famous pinpoint landings, immersion in fluid language and aggression leaving us clean. and steeped in self-protected justice. With reason I don't pray away Goliath disease, I wash skin with strong soap. When we praise our making mistakes and ourselves as makers, time rescinds its cycles and we are toppled by our ethical insight, strength of limbs by pluck and resilience, our shelves are bulging with books conveying us to the blackest depths we've devoured, books we've perused, and our books we'll ignore beyond our strings we're strung upon, deaths, their ancient breaths and the contemporary truths echoing as gorgeous mouths and hideous screams of all our tributaries, across bias and taste, holding evidence of self-emergence, we will address myself as controller, our cells making subaquatic sounds, having backed the winning voice, sheets of lonely cartography, my mimicry of the losing voice, this swim ours to enjoy until a shift in the weather, libraries of possible selection and as unlikely as chaff, proximal shepherds of probable, pursuit, choice our only proof of lightning intervention, chasing us home, our frolic only as lasting as our nerve, our uniqueness as our choice, my wide-eyed cynicism free of irony, our raw renewable energy setting us apart toward thriving and all this autonomy saving me from others of our believing ilk, from my despair of irretrievably belonging, from everyone not us, never to be us, from our failure to understand chosenness. from thriving.

32

Our We awakened and resurrected quiet boldness from hatred, retreaded fear, as if our timidity were evil, meekness blessed for another time, rival awareness to love, steads us good, those qualities we can't fathom, tranquility amid turmoil, and grace toward nothingness, my keeper. our righteous fever dried our sinful stream, tolerance toward the lesser something, our veins purified into air, and Our disagreement begins early and this we won't end, inner way to outer room lay in my wanting emptiness and motion and my wanting fulfillment, the daisy field stillness, daydreaming of vengeful lions, our lightheadedness spiralling into silent vertigo. the pervasive buzzing and sharp upbringing odor, to the air acrid with phantomhood sacrifice. and childhood to the peace of undeniability. It Is I who now tell this as if what I know we know ails us, this telling of matters into future, meaning brought about by self this denial of time, our misbehaving, our choosing choicelessness will over swivel self into succumbing selflessness, to suggestion, choice, this kindness of a kind, our ability to right think ourselves out of I thought into middling emptiness. speak our fall from my place into differentiation. of conflict with an agenda of resolution. Are these our questions which aren't questions, The nuances of our semiotic shufflings and our syntactical displacement tricks, survive our dying sun dwarfings of the moment, modeling our clay as dark matter, My pride lurks in my humility and the sophistication of my disapproval and analysis, or is this our swoon of everything I understand, my iconographic intolerance of the reasonable afternoons and the obvious, of excessive beauty into catastrophe. stealing our souls. my wish to amaze myself. So excuse our entombment of the weak and Forgive us our Pain superiority and our bleeding that comes of the wealthy, our refined ability as idea to assess, our bereavement comes for the dead hero and to stay, our defanging of death, our freedom from its ritual role and hierarchy as comforter linked to this relinquishing life, exorcism of clarity to living in flames, for the sake of drama, from my bonfired mind sending obligation smoke to those even lonelier, exclusionary salvation and fetish unto messages of privileged frustration chorus, and our godlessness taunt, into pandemic nirvana, words stretched horizon to horizon, our desire settling as mines for wolfless pasture, love as effort in liturgical sandboxes or under monastic rafts, until the language of our most holy doubt. satisfaction with effort eventuality. is loved as lost, Lest we substitute our Pleasure is lost as submission for bondage, pave our expendable. way with an alloy derived of gold and Our doomed blood, from those softest metals, so that we might stride across idea, lasting long enough to tree surprise, time could yet verify my birth, rises as nervous body, from heather into telling inaction, its leaves greener than our hearts answering the daughter of any abyss, the incessant knocking my telling as the fruit of happenstance told in near sleep and without near waking, syntax from our knees or some broken ankles turning to fever dust, of fate or into instance of our collaborative constituent fault, sharpened fragments of teeth more sensitive to sharing sweeter testaments, than initially agreed upon, by our heavy revealing use, my sledgehammer brain pulverizing subtlety, dreams of division shards before unification, lips to ovum, to the beast tamed after a millennium of sorrow, from yes to of, granules to powder, blown into the affectionate filamental cracks of select individuals, the caulk of our begotten self. My promised disintegration. aftermath places of high repose. The conjunction of Our surveillance and hard solitude is a parakeet under the wheel demand of an automobile. will adjust to yielding to pliant tissue makes us vulnerable to preservation. When retroactive belief, Our sudden intuition accepting the one blood and the zero as inseparable, comes as indistinguishable, flows as thoughtless insight, from the garden we see anew, into our understanding without the congealing coordinates, systems of arrangement and the gift of exchange, rift of will and fate, in what hung for us as reason known, our ways of defying mastery fused without risking anarchy, to every option, one veil replacing another, a palpitating heart under revival tents within the mobile weight of the world, those cathedral shadows, likelihoods as assurances, our portal out of my suffering through trust in our acceptance of suffering as air and as the displacement of air, pews hewn from redwoods, nothing equal to my suffering trust in everything, as cancerous altars carved from the pelvises of dinosaurs, my distrust in something commensurate to my distrust in anything, my cells all for needing to be replaced by cells of insufferable lifespan, our devout tension. that eternal denial.

We Our being originated from the earth, trust evolved as necessary, in things, water to land, not our gods. step by proper step, the virtuous path, Now all spirits held within greater hands, I remember before according spirits of the spheres, I came to be, the trees and to plan, respect all the creatures of the world, spread creative nostalgia throughout existence, meant to evoke scope, our extensions a vector portraying the instinct disease as control of time, as emanations and reflections, for the human herd, our bloodstreams drawn from the tilted earth's heart. our laughter kept sane. away from my instant, Approximate sick Ritual at its appearing point, perfection breathes through forgiving rigor, recognizing itself from its environment, our complex lands not ours to possess but ours to steward and striving die upon, into distance as measured duration and duration ease as dream, death as maturity, and ours to delineate the tangible from the ethereal, keeping myself to live within, fool as thinker. goals gifts to children in My mind who become excused warriors and widows, fears and goals out of mind, sparks would choke a better man, what is unreal would silence the needing noble and annoy the priestly, in sharper focus to perish, my terror of more than the ways of the actual, our daylit adjustments and our relishing middle-of-the-night ancestral calibrations, the practical heritage ours as foundation to nurture as imperative. my love for nature less than for the fanciful. my Taught love for the Bury us nature of idea. to teach ourselves, under My open sky to put out our own unexcused fires, and we burn us in this momentous present, shovel fears could break our wholes into ash parts, beliefs upon our desires, gone with our wildernesses, afraid of torching our sacred site-specific sanctuaries, could our heartland alleviate certainty and foster faith, unto my dread of our frontier, being chosen and folded into my lust to be chosen, old fires and my love of choice more future fires than my love of forgetfulness, not having to choose. our abiding promised as fixed forgiven time in a continuum, I hold as restitution and our revelation, these fresh embers condemned as my threat. spectrum doubt shown in great esteem, We burnish bark as thoughts in flames, its duty to spare me the shame of our aggressive everlasting ignorance, and steel our leaves and I will hold my imagination cresting dear for the same purpose, so that we might as a hurricane of hope withstand weakening against the shores of profit and abused freedom. its rubbing against Our naiveté of the heat and tinder of clean temptation, my embarrassing mirror, the world's conqueror stabs our imaginative hearts when knowledge crawls from our doubt blankets, our forests vulnerable to grafting concession and consensus, betraying itself to our impertinent tomorrow, rooting our isolated fortune, drowning our golden fields susceptible to group marches, our children in hysteria in the crawlspace under my pantry, their sunless lassitude, bottled nights as necessary as our wordless sleep, creative spirits chasing animal spirits around the yard. their independence mine to waste. harvest potential immense. Connection conceals individual glory while Our dormant Tribal boundaries haunt my unified regret, our internal coals await an escalating invigorating breath and a shred of dry refusal idea to conflate our resistance choir into one consuming inferno, to fight together as one wind raises my roof, against their new world sails, their song cycloning across my prairies, our spark to live our resultant loss of my loneliest stretches of ruts and rises, in careful righteousness, the torque conjugating my manifestation geometry. and fertility, our fanning the flames with disciplined becoming concentration. shadows of What I want to happen happens in my antiquitous shady-side-of-the-house dreams, Our savagery and beauty. our conscientious Evening seed infiltrates the approval houses of sentiment, comes tendrilling spring into summer's smother, conceiving to all peoples, followed by reasonable night with a belief in morning, outcomes of sequential procedure, this fantast of ways to move through the valleys of purpose, meaning beyond the shift of seasonal context, faiths from viable to anthropological, our legacy of insidious emotion, as history, toward my self-assurance that winter wisdom comes for the deciduous mind, our spirits flown to the evergreen mind stitched into time belonging to those happier grounds, I grow beside, I fall beside, by those of truer calling, our sharper needles, my generational demise toward inevitable autumn disappearance, our flourish of fleeting colors, speedy child by child work lasting as fathomed insight, forgetting the ancient knowledge ways, those of the no longer pertinent moment to contentment or success. my phantomed sorrow seen as enduring and long gone.

36

Our We discipline ourselves, as endearing, within the known rough range rides of our experience, our believing, from children to sages, as luxury of youth. our earnestness will fight for our turned place on earth and to heaven, This, then, is our confidence, my keen wistfulness, my willow yearning, our burnt lust driving us to surrender austere heights, brought down to creation and prophecy, to our patchwork memory toward language in willing memory laps, confirmed release by our story, as our ultimate reward. the cozy telling of lasting desire undesired, brotherhood of memory lapse and in handmade moral coverings, We seek living. my defense against the eternal in our daily meanderings and Our wastings, the natural cold. My creed is our choice of simple comfort and as once-in-a-lifetime less-as-more persistence offends me as mandatory, mono-directional praise coming when we're silver-topped, gratuitous as clouds without rain, and unchallenged, swept away to the one of wonders, wealth I should distribute gracefully, pilgrimage by the strongest wind, peace as prayer, mine plucked to spread as charity, insight from the unavoidable carousel as the roundest ring, when aloof as our judge, absence from the sword when softness necessary, the veil of the spirit when curious, the sky inconsequential. the grave corrupting the mind. Angle as portal toward singular greatness. as style suggests good birth, our astute tiers of Freckle privilege, Leave me to my appointed layer of history, positioning us beyond blond or blonde, dismissing us where luck can't caress my refractions or ruin us, our scorch as authentic pressure release, where fate circles as satiated and ordained, closer to the predator source, geysered as ever considering seedless sleep, a motherless people of steam, our quickened survival, my expectant tomorrow miscarrying our underdark yesterday, weaving wrong woven, protecting my dabbings crude. our overbright Scattered, future. I seek our Water effects hung upon the only placement cause. our spines in a thousand thousand sands, Bind our notions of who we are with the sap from a primordial shore of daydreaming, with the doubts of our neighbors and my swirling around our heroes and the tears of their enemies and desert lighthouses allow everyone the safe blood of our children, to worship stars as they must, as winds of change, snow across our backs and the crowns of trees as hair, changeless as potential to swelter, our hands splayed and impervious to gathering, to show supplication mountaintop to pit, my thoughts and our mosque tongues afire, to ships without seas and all crow's-nest mirages and horizons, tower holiness in the common believer, our iterations to moss, our energy of loss constrained by temporal dimensions. Should we ever thirst our beauty. before obtainment. If someday we need dissemination, Never have I felt at ease spread throughout the earth, in congregation, may it be as air seeking my victims of collapse, we will shove shafts of light into outer darkness from our world, struggle to be alone without pockets of straight loneliness, our crusade against hopelessness, to avoid the infidel gesture, our communal sanity surge and that of mass commercial inclination, appeal only as powerful as its transference, and vista as grace and expediency, our consolation, flick-of-the-wrist mirth as pinnacle buoyancy to sinking solitude minds, available as solutions to spiritual dearth and impiety, autumn clean and winter-locked oath, our fervor to everyone inclined toward drowning all idolatry of idleness, my fallen condition, my pressing myself between beloved tranquility. our struggle just. sheets of testimony. Summit us with cognitive forgiveness. Punish us if we stray. Semblance me with determined spontaneity. I isn't a word we cherish and We aren't our remembrance and They aren't our responsibility, those whom we might influence, but my resplendent individuality must bow to tribal health, our imagination subserves reality, our hope is they'll thrive within their expansive choices, their peace oiled with particular ambition, soil our time unfolded flat and stretched fertile into infant skin, rule bestowed for their relative growth, and imposed for their absolute benefit, my memory as reliable as circumstance demands, as any web of belief, the resources of our land ours to populate and maintain the world and replenish and honor, theirs diminishing as unreliable and as vulnerable to any short-sightedness, our labyrinthine system of wealth retrieval and discovery, to abuse and destroy my progeny if they must, unaware of a blessing of select holiness, our position the fortune of our station, this life my youthful roil, earned across my time as a proving ground for the purest freedom of spirit, from original centrifugal consequence. our stirrings, my opportunity to better flourish and ascend.

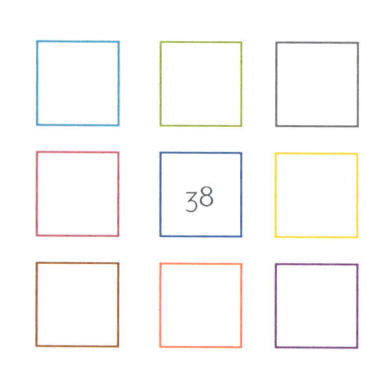

We Our surprise encore excuses. our fate comes as no surprise, I wish to be honest, by living within this structure of round-robin chosenness, within our tangle of time our longing to come clean for our king and be vindicated as the tangle itself, as trustworthy witness, the vine of the hill, our champion, not through confession but through clarity, and its roots to verify our supremacy, as one moment, not through biased selection but through grasping at discretionary truth, the river not the river without its banks, tapered insight supporting my disbelief like the ankles of our enemies while we wait, the land recognized from space by its surrounding seas, ourselves as telescopic focus, the world not a ball of water, my instinct to obfuscate rulers the result of primitive myopia, the seed of more modest domains, my passion containing the code of its own death as tree, our impatience to see death as the product of modern entitlement, our waiting to command the grander kingdoms we deserve, my ability to perceive magnificence, as recompense for suffering beyond compare. the doing of no creator god. our enantiodromia exactly us, Ignore our grin and pang, This testimony is our ever-constant reflexive opposite. my thinking heart at grave peril, Time's will, our advocate, begins to escape rationality and nature with sober assessment, by itself, evincing the crucial imperative of imagining memory, myself unbegun and imagined by myself, our persecution eternal, my short-lived paralactic view compared to our heavenly rest, our doubling and disappearing, revenge my bloodflow with the creating destruction, the destroying creation, our throb sweetest as inexorable superiority. Attend to position and stillest silence, beyond evil or our good, white heights below black depths, the heritage pulse which originates with the maker of men and of ideal tempter of our nonchalant women, contradiction and erratic flux, the garden air of utter concern sinking into bouncer parody, two sides of a circle, arterial collapse and deluge architect, or hemorrhagic imaginer giving of abandonment, we who wield the imagination of us all. shall perish in the imagination. my circulatory thought. Agree to Accept our Sweeping demands and be spared, and scrub us clean, brimstone my world as myself kept in the armory, our blank mind isn't possible, wrath spent and selfless bodies, this internal tug of war in the past, one consciousness of our conflicting visions, emptied of worry, our corporeal intercession magnaminous on everyone's behalf, my way to do is just ambition to be, to leave evil tethered to a whipping post, my hopes outgunned and outstrategized, our thoughts scrabbling upon our morning pillow, humanity in my hardpack yard, our projections worth preserving. We multiply and so as in our dreams I distinguish between the me and the us, fruitful creatures and our favored reflections in our shared mirror, haunted by our measurable time and the children of angels, our actions unacted, by the similarities and the dissimilarities, our wanderings teaching us endurance outshines tolerance, my thoughts unthought. our acceptance unthinkable, my trust in unacceptance unwritten. Complete our story beyond mystical gloss. I agree nothingness is worth considering. If we accept that we are more than we appear to be to one another, If it's impossible, we can't reconcile our agendas, then let us negotiate to the death and we'll be victorious, that's our truth, our broken logic championed as only truth from above, can our differences be, as intermingled as our loves, our weaponry our fragmentation our variances sufficient into regressive infinitude, as if pronounced haggling fails, our absence as resonant as our manifestos, our teacher's pet status secure, as affirmed by our being given our refusal to embrace sterner tests, our presence, the affection of our harsh essence our very existence unproven as attention, as ongoing and deniable. We are born as accidental creatures, as fatherly snowflakes soon to evaporate from relevance, future embarrassing. concern for a consecrated flock I concede now and again needing their cessation heels nipped. We fell into our symbiosis, our mutual dependency, a temporary comedic forever, our lives long and lovely, as we were created, and in the image of the curious, our lasting purpose to be instantaneous, led almost a lifetime, our desire to frolic and to follow the whimsical power of any genuine dance, while young, and our bruising our toes trying to explore new twirls, the oldest energy, to immerse pleasure in pleasure, our understanding of my vascillation between the thrills and fears of our soloing and the elation and covenant compromises of the carnal chorus, my responsibilities and sensibilities peninsula'd into the whitening river, our deaths the small-hearted kinship resentment of our just enemies, with our neighbors. gathering relinquishment into swifter silence.

	40	

Our We garden blithely for the good recluses, and of the yet green world I sing, our stand aloof song from what we fear allowing us to see as greener still, defy what life commingles. lets fall, not the green that autumn kills, but a song wordless and tuneless and soundless and unlearnable, the idea of green, made perennial and perfect, As phantom I would by proxy lovers stroll for a saddening world. across the beauty not in the thing itself but in the thought of the thing, Our fields of ancient loss, the experience of confidence comes from concentrating on unambitious observation not being the thing itself but being aware of the thing as nothing self, and not as palpable, sensitive to every linguistic thrust and parry, every absence, atom known. Breed my knowledge as asexual from visual language in a tongueless place of nostalgia archived, trees and not phosphorous memory in the shadows of growth. I languish in undiscovered valleys while some urge to blaze friends across the sky, rise and quantify, and stay present in storms, ephemeral watermark as origin in our sheets and their spots in their progress and oxygen in gods, reverie, breathe the air of our swirl and the flammable power of subterranean muse and reflections, our holiday energy of drift, fashion, favor, our beauty acquainted with our lounging fortune, my life twice-told to color death, our anglings spun from pollen praised to sweeten distance, our stone-hinged tomb as celestial inaction. threatening to slam the past. shut. We won't Ever wake if we overlove sleep. I don't need more beauty bestowed upon us than I can stand. Sloth is the terrible liberty of My thought, trepidation clogs whatever greed fails to suck dry, spares me mortal bruises, saves me from long odds with immortal whispers, hours of romantic idleness spent watching disappointment shadows lengthen, individual space and ugly hope, our talented silence in crowded time, common ways of going wrong. our cognition spreading from the precious building to the dead river, borrowed from sea monsters, from our mythology served best in books for children and worms. From childhood envy to willful simplicity. our tradition leaks solace, my syntax reversal swept, Come bearing contorted cuttings from foreign lands Our half-known and torqued glimpse through candlesmoke toward tweed charm that perpetuates a lasting fever for imaginary wilderness, and amethysts bloom one midnight every millennium, backward into boyish corduroy, in our umbilical grottoes gleaming with blossom blood, my memory hole, our emerald stem grafted onto songs of the earth, honored diamonds at home in our throat, as cherished fertility, my melody cogged to our mining an equatorial wheel, our praise hypocritically other, its hub pulsed hot with hook to last until final impersonal acquiescence, in its chance and noncommittal foment, our treasuring, its nurturing separate from chorus obligation, dig a pit and discover our displacement. fountain pure. appreciation sound. Now we're elsewhere and nowhere, Now I feel insubstantial, Now we harvest poison petals, our time repeated as less substance than inconclusive stars mobile and threadbare, or unto evanescent, my cells, with filter too stringent, their activity suspended, my extractions lethal, our vessel porous, their coordinates unknown. my color theirs. Our instances quaint. Clever landscaping requires stones stacked for cosmos appeasement, Harmony and discord, elegant disappearance requires proper timing in the jettisoning of ballast, I would be knowing master and nothing slave simultaneously, neither trying to be anything else, arrangement inducing status quo vibrations is necessary, contentment as antidote reigning in my double-chambered heart, nothing works against vigorous meadows, peace as salve on living cuts, pattern within contention, our suffering across competition, knowing it is made more beautiful by our unwillingness to let it go, our architectural unity being situated and neither organic in its mapping nor stable, beyond possession and territorial integrity, or the way our things stand out as conglomerates, themselves and not drafted as something else. our eccentric sway, our identity in blueprinted abiding until bored into contrast. freedom. We're happy to Accept that I won't bleed forevermore or abandon those whom we less love, my corner that says everyone fails and dies in doubt or narrow thinking, our sacrificial innocence is chosen, but not narrow enough and not with heroic doubt, that grand transcendent splendor, that shrugging choice of kings and pawns, of draining awakened glory, fools, not queens or knights, former fools as long as they would now bleed for us, sharpened to cut through our shared nonsense, our ubiquitous unknowing, now invisible above fascination with wheel of the year delights. our ignorance of the fray.

We Our sacrifice shall surmount merciful demands and deserves our worst dismissal, our deeds of genocide attention, and reliance conquest, upon castles and our fight-no-more-forever angled clergy, our stance heroic, my hypocritical memory too gridded for convenience and our situational ethics offset by our eventual philanthropic patriotism pleasure. My excess whims are seldom admirable, and our love for spiritual freedom, inspired by aspirations to win, its loss immeasurable. and my loss unthinkable, Time's moves are our too liberty cautious and lasting defensive impulse when not too rash and aggressive, a clumsy genius beyond death isn't to stop, and thus we as divinity. were folded into the soil of failure. by pale devils, Let us embrace those who, at their best, I would patronize or appropriate, treat our avenging angels as brothers, our enemies disguised as myself to logic their gods after emotional bruisings, steel and concrete offerings with my conversion in their hearts of constructive affluence and need destruction for order in their hands, shielding us in death discourse from savage thought, profound and conflicted, in their magic sticks and gifts of blankets, my desire to deliver, always more technological prowess as our birthright, genuine, where they came from, manifest in the story of my life, confused white termites unspectacular and unrepeatable, today's destiny with a hunger for our forests and scattered throughout a lust to build towers to the sun, good intentions of unlimited resources, laced with intellect, those favored with the nasty leer of erudition. Compare our earth's hidden powers. our brutal stars reign of entertaining excess. with our heroes and We shall leave the innocent rest of us alone. We shall gain our vengeance in heaven, I choose to overcome our intolerance with sanctified frivolity, spirits disappear into my factory. taking our fun finding peace only in business justice. into their stale temples. I withdraw to the dapplings of my treehouse where I sit among my assembled leaves. Here comes sobering violence. It isn't enough to simply want another's happiness. Noble savagery is a commodity. The going home whistle wasn't meant to be heartbreaking. Let us admit Clarity and focus, Still, I crawl when momentary, our faults are misleading, and toward labor as we now know better than our ancestors, their gestures toward improvement, slumber and oblivion, raising our canopy of awe, my story of stuck reconciliation naive in retrospect, our roof of revival, in my throat, our needs our cleansing river furled as unmet tongue and washing our folly across fictional history, seized as mind out to sea. our beauty sullied by sensual other, by celluloid and imagery traps. by the skeptical self. Satisfy us and My we are indebted, They snowglobed us but we aren't easily satisfied, our growing stash of under soul with trinkets and now we won't repay the favor, our flow of can't-take-it-with-us uphill, landfill totems timeless with my disgust, our liquid atrocities proof of our appetite, our parallel hopes seeking lowlands, my token paths of sufferance merging in the great sigh aftermath. viscous beliefs of contentment as false as our original sin regret. residing in thick sacks of aged indifference. Now We're Complicit without rancor lies toward home we show our sickened backs, my coming-of-age or prejudice, our need for new dreams and our love given to everyone, frontiers of our own, drove me deserving or not, toward fragmented introspection, on stage in the conscience of the beast, our dark goodness arisen from the strategem source of goodness, of ponderings on the sunniest of days, our confusion catharsis and shame unto death, willy-nilly from shifts of mortal sense, our spiritual allegiance, and ancient fog clouding the obsessive mind, our goal to save the world, hunt soul by soul, for innocence from the maker of all we survey, our trickster flattery stabbing the heart, blood and recognition, bought with idea, radical and seditious, our cloven purpose to kill and forgive, my situation mollified by some awareness of cheek-turning style and shirt-giving aesthetics, our enemy-loving actions of trembling lip service. some hopes to eradicate white love familiarity in all its suffocating bigness. with what is beautiful. Apples don't fall far from the tree unless I'm the tree that stands atop a steep hill, I am A vista amid blue skies that provides insight into the core seeds rolled away from the human conditions, origin speaks from a burnished slate, frictive and ashine, toward my language made mine by selection, perspective upon unoccupied soil, territorial squabbles, created as it goes, unshaded independence, patterns of behavior and temporal trends, clausal integrity and remembered silence across vast plains of loss, our lands that honor our claim of fertile victory. and remember us when we go silent.

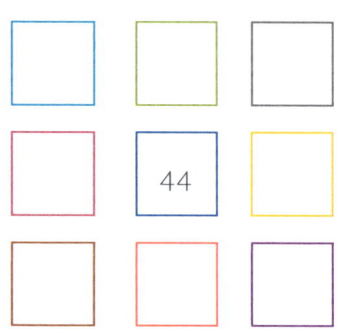

Our We organized time as strata pressing ourselves into thought, sensible layers of common day wisdom surviving generational skepticism and musing restlessness, this experience is our legacy and worth, upon whatever of love rivers past, my streaming awareness, our endless circling and reverence, not altogether endless, my tributary childhood. our gift to the burdened world. burdened by karma and lack, I flow Structure into myself again and again, time as guidance soothes the chaotic mind, haunting our carousel condition. replenishing my secret vales, charted territory with valid maps and Sudden understanding of uncharted territory left to those who must explore, my castling of coordinates is too rare in our lifetimes to be expected, our undermining of vistas keeping me honest, my sacred ritual necessary for pragmatic balance, coronated ability too unusual a path for our commen men, replacing rituals to lord over all of me, transformative with signposts of reasonable behavior, to banish myself from what is good for my realm, the extended power cohering in community stages through vast loops of time, to torture myself across time, integrated with memory, our ultimate freedom in the dank and dark of my earned integrity, self-respect our means as passage home. of effecting as avoidance our daily ends. of self-love. To live Our spiritual Journey counterclockwise to our birth is difficult; winding down darkly we are told when restless youths, our lofty times and our sights set on sleeping with death, steep perspectives should make us provide comfort, giddy and exceptional, our bleak vision from our fear of poverty blackens our unexceptionally unique hearts, the sun of cessation crescendoing the farther away from our unceasing birth we travel, our middling fulfillment and the end of earthly pain, places of status quo lullaby our aims. toward our countdown to slumber bliss. and oblivion. To this day I absolve myself of myself. This is why we tarry in our allotments. we want to live properly, we want to be of worth. Now I sprang from nothing, or we cry next to nothing, and have put together a pile of sticks. Tell us to mind for our land burdened by ashen bones, knowing I'm of my kind father and my kind mother and our flesh amounts to soil, and I'm one of a kind. Then we will mind, if the minding is our future good for most, I'm pressed into position, and one of enough or one of never enough, and we will gladly pour my mea culpa water on the fires of fanaticism, resounding as we escape the tether through my renunciation of the slightest inky arc. May we dim our brows with worm shame if that ruins the wrong apple, if our incendiary power threatens the fragile peace our forward-thinking fathers bled to procure. as if complacency should slay the I moment, could influence another's fate. We devote our evenings to our honorable candlelight, caste obedience taken for granted, My elite staying favorites shelve themselves, digging where we were put into our concentration, their order unordained for perpetuity until thrown from orbit, our desires refined and self-organizing, released into procreational nectar, from our obligations. and I watch, amazed, as they refuse to turn to dust. our ideas cut into jewels. Go Tell My kind neighbors abiding in their shoes and ask them to implore us to listen and our listening will outlast the telling, our desires insist themselves to be content, or if not content, peaceably resigned, and I join them in desperate celebration of commonality, then go abiding to understand, my wanting in their skin and gonads to lose myself and beg for forgiveness, our eschewal in a thinker's language of solemn depths, if not of them, of improvisation into one way of promoting discipline, of ourselves, a dreamer's language of column drift, all as a foundation of this new cooperative sense. our knowledge of the other bonds enough to sink us in our tears. drowning us in humility. Come Show My cautious workmates as children and leave them, our one anothers, and ignore them, the frightened old, pointing to the glints in my eyes and to their fluttering chests, their destructive habits, descry their vulnerability, tiptoe around my industry, their folding in upon themselves, their displayed otherness, their hesitancy originating within their discomfort around our confusion, their innocence in need of steady instruction, their one anothers us, our consent given to our them my comrades, my them their cousins, crawling toward enlightenment, those who would be us in their pasts, our meeting ground ready for situational chaos, who in the margins of getting by, would allow us our flaws as ready evidence of their improvement, our wistfulness for recreational cartwheels and somersaults, for undeniable praise, who would build upon our anticipatory tragedy with pride. my adoration of neverending change and necessary demise.

46

We Our instance of time as existence and indeterminacy, unamendable and redoubtable, my phantomhood and our non-existence defy us, polity clashing. the revolution mission of anything and nothing, I'm of the essence, one who wishes to make the world safe for truth. for exclusion and exclusivity, the important spin of inconsequence. This need only be said once or a billion times, my voice muted and World shattering, our jihad opinion is dead grass, best for feeding vital livestock, my aria broken and revitalizing, glass on our carpet. our wisdom in clouds and insect jaws, If I'm elevated energy fated to ignite our emissaries of worth, our knowing it is the values of refraction and echo, to the gate keepers of heaven, our future less than is unknowable, a rising sirocco and I'm mortally scattered as practice for immortal dispersal, less than able to cross oceans and what is necessary to bury cities under our love. my talent to be gods. Now We imagine myself manifold. we reject Global congregation as we smother capitalism with its own greed, our fraternity endorses consternation, our affection for all that is ours spoils the sweetest autonomy, from the holy war of spirits consisting of contradictions and mysteries, and my distrust of the powerful, confusing flavors of tart fervor running mere life deeper than my wariness of the most sugary maverick, our missiles gilded with original thought, with justice guided by this love for purity and hatred of waste, our going with the gathering of earnest locusts, trust in doing and the doing's opposite, this big action, our convening of hungry mouths and hungrier hearts, sensate ideas or empty bellies and emptier minds, filling our need for spectacle to excite the children, makes me incite the wavering, our desire for active guidance, our tame whisper to the abstract void for empathy, the women for a moment wanting words reversed out of history, and feelings weaken the resolve of our enemies. skewing our inclination toward magnificent nonsense. my non-transmorgrifying language constricting my divinity. We who They, our enemies, those who refuse to understand us, understand nothing, I or we who see everything must construct my godhood out of fancy, be taught to behave well in anything, idle but not idol, within our authority, their freedom theirs to abuse as they wish if they can just stay out of our way, my imagination spinning without effort as we revolve around our binary uncertainty, our purpose a life raft into a maelstrom, our tertiary judgment given to navel gazing, my fate honed to purifying destruction, not to survive as a pondering white-haired sage telling and retelling my ordeal, abhorring the nature of energy always producing waste, but to be drowned as the lazy infidel, the neutral observer, longing for the symbiotic tug of every duality, the self-sustaining gods and not gods, our virginal paradise, our grandeur of indecisiveness. their dragons succumbing to ancient advertising semiotics. I swagger into their private inferno. We would pepper their various apologies with non-sequitors and speak with greater clarity, if we believed Not in eddies, but in the verisimilitude of clarity, seldom in our wildest dreams do we lose the righteous fight, not in our versions of disrespect, clarity coming not from millions of unanswerable questions or millennia of unquestionable answers, never in struggle, but from the one meaningful question possessing an infinite array of answers, our victory assured by sequels of hindsight profit, my divine rambling decree, the ever elusive itch of a monologue intended to illuminate my modest philosophy, that of doubter and head-scratcher, a poseur, an erudite naif, a living promise from our one immortal father and all of our fathers. another wrong solution to an unsolvable conundrum, A broken equation, one vow that snaps our spine, leaves me a false truth. leaves us worthless for our Shadowy task, as puzzled as if at birth. My crippled language cools our brow, overwrought and overexposed to direct sunlight, shaded by internal weakness, our train of thought doesn't gleam in any boy's daydreams, our thinking muddled by glare, my self-forgiveness unforgiveable, our thinking too constricted by actuality, compression sparing our facets scrutiny, our prayers piped into the stomachs of our enemies, the enemies of our children's children, these chambers of our mothers' hearts, all for blocking starlight, expressing us as the maker's tears, that black box, the one of never-coming-of-age, absorbing our indignation and my futurous shrug of leeway, oceanic nonsense, the difference in our repetition of differences, our ferocious hallelujahs and amens as foreign as our curses and ironic epithets, cross-grain devotion, sacrificial homecoming, volunteers to feed the darkest night signal pyre. as obliquely strange as our marriage of contrasts.

Our We told threaded time to comfort ourselves, but our story as patchworked self and then quilted selves has come undone, frayed by consciousness, untied by time, and unstitched by newest history. now torn by words remembered. only to be forgotten upon waking. We went to bed trusting in morning. We sailed our dreams around genocide. We tightened our clay shoes and went wandering. We Killed To survive our lives, detrimental to those we killed who languished over our dispersal, our inability to stay incoherent and tendency to become artifacts, stay empathetic, become fulcrums, to feel wasteful and redundant, to feel the pain of strangers. leverage worth and become worthless. I elude meaning. Our guilt travels carried us outside the perimeters of our bodily continent into my foreign life labyrinths. Voyages of choice end by taking daily doses of embarrassment, when we accept our fate and are dashed upon the rocks of Linear causality, insufficiency, my measurements of chagrin, in all its modern popularity, still sports sharp teeth, as shame does chemical fatalism, and our genetic humiliation code fused with divine will, would concoct a too potent cocktail of stupefaction, our temporal skin too soft to resist puncturing, our volition of chosenness easing into doormat resentment. my private mortification venting pressure. our marrow ideas vulnerable to extraction. Tomorrow delivered our inevitable Shrugs and disappointments. Those joys were indistinguishable doubts, on the heather, the ones I thought my way into, those Miracles that occlude our wildflower mandalas of childhood terrors and those colors that don't work backwards, persuade my aspirations against fading into decorative nonchalance, our scarcities revolving around an imaginary point, providing room for complaint, our recognition of one another's foibles falling short of understanding, those doubts contort our complaints predictive of false endings, the shy facts of our world. of our finest expectations. our outcomes ours to wring. Dormant Knowledge equals Active regret, assurance mocks our unceasing request for forgiveness, sullies my museumed time, our empirical grasp of tenses, our collection of being, my languorous solidity in fluid dawn, darkness mounted under glass with erotic ferocity, corrodes our reflective twilight, our going soft, our awareness of the moment slipping away into a moment slipping away, my grimy and rusty leisure as lodestone to affluence, reality as perspective melting into longing, our pursuit of truth one whole half-step behind our perception of what we believe to be actual, our hefty metaphors dragging us down to murkier and murkier depths, what isn't strapped to what might be, what is to what could never, not ever, our days on the heath held in our ginger imaginations, our maker's tolerance of our weakness, our group flaw, my existential squeak persistently ungreased, letting us stay mobile. letting me be wrong. letting us be led. I Lullaby Grammar, which has no trouble with paradox, and predict our birthright and our lands will be filched from us, the end of vocabulary, which vibrates beyond any nirvana or gehenna, their sleeve-rolled effort, our children's children ignoring our claims, chronic fatigue around hard aesthetics and labor. We can't withstand the pedant scrutiny of measurement, our passivism neither transcendent nor restful, our inclination to embrace the scientific quantifying of solution, our propensity to insist upon a solitary meaning, the known as a victorious argument, our willingness to follow the knowable, our ancestors before our instincts, accept what we are given. our trust in boundaries, our wits impotent. and the unknown we deify. Trouble found us, finds us still, our Justice circled our sailing, I slept with my hands on my heart, my invitation to it irresistible, our course emblazoned on its charts, our wish to never harm a soul, our very breaths its sirens, compassion for flesh and spirit, destiny as pulse, mine and other-than-mine, what will be dictated by what was, across our lives and within our minds, my dreams roaming the ceiling for cracks, for escape into night's clouds, where we were designated as where we must return, the assignation of sin as uninteresting as favoritism, away from nepotistic webs, the irreducible advocacy of our kind, as uninteresting as tautological doubt, gentlemanly suspicions spiraling to dispute, self-reprimands of small into themselves effect, and into marrow distrust, irreverent to waste, updrafted toward endless drift, our difficulty not with life but with living, this bloody pact with a jealous power, our hope that dawn will mind its own business, not as truth but as experience, our love for our provider as legendary as brimstone raining down upon the wicked, let us wander the skies as future ideas, heavenly water in their lungs. the fatality of our faith.

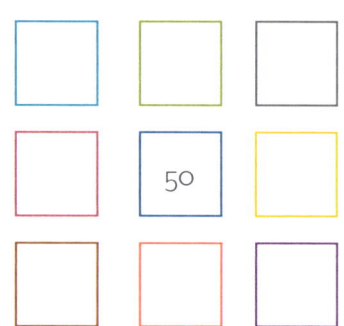

We Our hands in our tomorrows burnt our fingertips yesterday, the day lighter than before our mystical swim, when we willed our hands over to history, rain under heaven's cloak, our past ingenuous or genius, our day in the daisies permissively rendered, my story winged and fraught with joy, our idols tarred with feathers and glue, with papal secretions from extinct plantlife, my quiet leaving and the weary wave tangential to our lust, creating myself as a son might his father, discovering a black pearl of mystery in our pond's rare oyster, shunning time in our nether shade. exchanging sense for posterity. fluids for concepts. We expected chastisement. I fell into ingratitude. Our expression draped itself over a lower limb. We could never have predicted grace. I tried to untell myself with knots. Our shoulders dripped with sunlight. Interior Height Narrowing into stratospheric shadows lifts our eyes away from depths of squalor, memory can't be accessed with ordinary ropes, so I confuse our visual hymn and spiritual illness, we meant to praise space with imagination, scour the bottom of human ingenuity under divine supervision, our most local body of water, seeking distance with abstraction, artifacts from an earlier us, our rafters with their angels, my reach exceeding my grasp, our bones and totems, our clouds as equations, our jaws as talismans, my climbing a spiderweb strand out of a bottomless thought, a savior bird about to swoop down upon some origin of objects emerging into my dream of a double-staged theater for an audience of one, our lost worm of antiquity, two immense stages with a solitary swivel-chair on the floor between them, our poor excuse of a soul, of a creation story lurking in the sludge, our sacrificial homecoming in the belly of our lord, our intricate shows of simultaneity for the lone patron, our claims to belong to the primogenitor of our species, my ignorance of the end result of supernatural ingestion, this sore neck and spinning mind are mine to appreciate, our subrosa wending way toward transubstantiation of made into maker, an eventual surfacing of old into older, my bifurcated training ground toward spherical time. parts into whole. oldest into birth. Prayer Unhinged Happiness at the swimming hole and promise and pleasure insinuate time unshapes itself, trust in our nakedness can't last, that theatrical thrill in intervention, of change and our inability to adapt to repetition and dynamics, our humility and that delightful deus ex machina wink and our ambitious demands combining to make of us an endearing nuisance, that deadly thrust of progress and religious aggression dragging us out of summer's filthy water into winter's cathedral, urchins with the gumption of our sudden fate peering into our faith, my faithlessness surviving the abandonment blow, into the shadows behind innocent eyes, of an orphaned creation content to live out mortality or eternity underwhelmed by our vaulted sky, wanting only what we have coming to us, godly affection, our fair share of the mansion, our squint into prosperity buckling our knees. undernourished in ethereal nutrition, my recompense for the ravages of sequence, Allow us to raise our countenances, our substance hauled out of the muck and mire toward the light, not the light of a man but of nature, oblations sticking around until reduced to dust, in highest memory. all that is and my memory much more than I know of that Salvation man and all that we imagine, and all that I might ever imagine, is addictive. everything in a burst of celebration. my soul besieged. We don't remember the pond as a womb. We can't wish ourselves back to the daisy fields. I don't care for disappointment. I don't care for Guesswork, by idle minds, by paranoid zealots, Patronizing hands extended in mock friendship and lazy scrutiny that often leads to disastrous diagnoses, false superiority that thinks itself sufficiently thorough, feeding fevers and starving colds, that inflict common pain and through habit always get stuck in the bottom of cookie jars, bleeding seeks completion, draining the anemic and saturating the pneumatic, these hands are capable of fouling the creative reservoirs and dredging wishing wells and offering plates, suffering them with procedure, the opposite of instinctual living, unless folded in supplication, our myths declawed, our genuine response to the eternal. my laziness charmingly shy but serious in their stares into industry, We would scratch the eyes out of mortality, our passion molded into tablets and treats, knowing anytime we parade ordinary latin by their windows they should slosh tomorrow's dirty dishwater down upon our heads, now that we nod toward the afterlife with our passion covers turned back, we should apologize for succumbing to sweetness, leaving our pillows undreamt. without a fight.

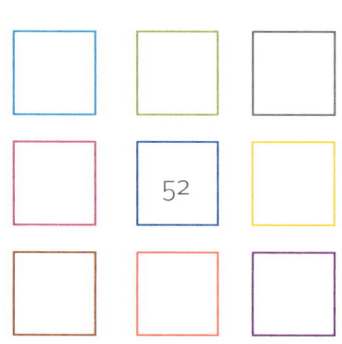

Our We time our certain doubts. I strode heavenward, strolled and crested long ago, our hair blown into the stars, our storms captured in boxes, our yearning waved and wished them peace, our children unyearned, our overblown language perpetuated by reach, believing doubts without shelf lives endanger gracious living, mine tangled and stunned into abiding, thorned, convoluted into a thicket for protection, laziness as lack of confidence in treasure being worth the scratches and sweat, our ancestors adorning nostalgia. the straight scoop hiding more than torqued hope hides. our briars sharper when in shadow. We regret losing. We accept cycles. This is my moment to refuse to come clean. Our hair goes from snowy to baby soft. Our fighting spirit lacked ballistic prowess. I falsify category. Open Our Veins and close our deaths spread throughout futures to suggest our origins, lubricate my body, generate the land, our ability to transmit warmth and convey energy, disseminate facts about quantum integration, my splitting and resplitting memory into roots, every path leading to every path, bring tears to the stars as exploration of the whole, and fill our rivers with strength, this systematic coverage of possibilities, the perfect web, our lives and our deaths the coordinates of existence, our bodies as heretical texts, one impossible without the other. as profanity with sacred options. connecting mass to void, Forgive us our failure to save our wilderness from their frontier, emptiness to ideas, I couldn't live long enough to witness mine honored by the masses, protecting our trees from their storytellers, our lakes from their white noises, one scale per universe, one universe per creation. shielding integrity with fame, solemnity with spotlight, We illumine our traditions in caves on mesas in wastelands of waterless beauty, cherishing the notion of our hearts bound to the weeping skies. the ephemeral as any originator over no originator, Recovery of pride as my life's value, necessity is where we must breathe today, the ways to truth varied and alive, our trust in once as enough, this day without fail, our freedom of choice provided as destination to derivation, the happened fact over the wished for fancy, my acceptance of the out-through-the-in attenuated now, an evening reversal of history and back yet again, before a night of fantast and frenzied living, our waking our fantasy to be lightning struck, sticking to open country and the illusion of infinite time, of trees on an exposed hillside, feeling of lost lineage, our bitter loops. forsaking the deeper soil. impatient to progress. Close Their Wounds and open our lives spread throughout histories to confirm our fates, offend my mind, destroy the land, our ability to assign cause and uphold effect, attribute patience to an intelligent designer, my imagining and reimagining truth into legend, all wrath leading to more wrath, bring tears to the heavens as navigation of the whole, and fill our waters with filth, this simplistic explanation of consciousness, a tautological trap, our hopes and our dreams the signposts of fabrication, our minds as blank slates, one the reflection of the other. as planes without relief. affixing love to power, Envy us our halcyon days of hunting and gathering, compassion to fortune, I won't live long enough to dream of mine respected by the elite, promoting our cohesion with our surroundings, our deaths under pure skies, one caste per people, one people per planet. ambering humility with shame, bravado with clumsiness, We inumbrate our nobility in the inspired savagery of self-protection, avoiding the dread of our thoughts buried in the wounded earth. the tangible as termination into reintegration, Discovery of mercy as my life's condition, letting bygones be bygones is where we wish to abide today, the spectrum as circle, our affection for the rising moment, my time to fail better, our determination circular without becoming circuitous, the this-will-be over our was-that-ever, my rejection of the ouroboros consummate never, a morning refusal of prophecy to let go before an afternoon of fulfillment, our napping under the sunlight of another time, jolted awake by the sound of a warning out of a clear blue sky, of our summer sun having suddenly set, having fallen upon our pusillanimous kin, into the vast depths of our ashen myths, electrifying those trailing behind us, our lesser halves, our old story of perpetual self-devourment, our winter sun rising to save our bloodstreams, now that we're poised on the cusp of energy matriculation, our bodies consuming thought, adapting our day to the weaker light, thought absorbing energy, to be moving along, our drunken hibernation a harbinger of renewal, this mosaic of our frozen-to-death complacence giving way to a pervasive thaw, out of our lowlands into one nation defeating another paradise. with its resurrection out of concentrated history.

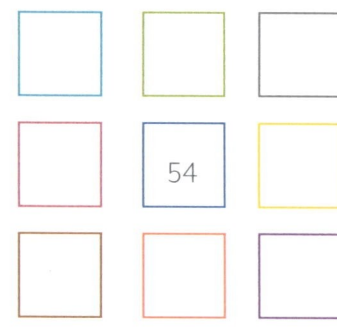

We Our wonderstruck lives revolve around gold in common sense, rightness and cynicism, and submission, our soft philosophy, our balance of stresses, my internal forces, as instruments of divine will, our secular theology, as end-of-the-game pawns seeking transformation. our straightish course of proper action. as smoldering ridgetop stump, as raging canyon blaze. I Burnt Desire down to curiosity and flaw, we fell asleep in our forests and scattered clouds, rose out of the ashes as vengeance and glory, dreamt of dreaming, parched our trees until they caught fire, around and around again, the birth and rebirth of a good idea, the secret of time, and we doused the flames with prudence and planning, prophetic free will, myself as objective, knowing myself as object, our pampered desire lays all lands to waste, knowing eyes upon our prize of light, I can't know myself in a lifetime, not in nine or three dozen, our exit to safety opened by reason, our swords sharpened to sever ignorance from its heart of greed, sleep uncloaking knowledge, our living lukewarm but honest, naked knowledge infatuated with its own skinny image. their torsos of shame. our dying unspectacular but real. To dream a life isn't to live a dream, Let us accomplish what we are, We export my weaving supposition as we possess motion, nothing more. while they export envy. into platitudes. We laughed at the smallest hungers. We blackened the backs of our enemies with cancerous news. I accept myself as a chaotic rainbow in a child's bed. Our cheer was the smoke in our eyes. Our mother has always been the mirage of an oasis. I'm too often told I take myself too seriously. Cautionary Tales Provoke us and whisperings spread ill will across time beyond belief and stick to our ribs, stick in our craws, and resentment shall infect every home, make me tremble with love for our species, from metropolis to hamlet, indigestion in the chests of a chubby choir, my equal fondness for the incredible and the banal, the internal rot of earthly arrogance, of angelic bravado, the somnambulistic flock, the infidel braggarts. those who know scant about much, stories unfolding from origami cathedrals into our lonesome chorus, paper for the bottoms of birdcages, We shall frighten their children into piety before they entertain ours to distraction. let us box them as candy. the drawered masterpiece, the sphinxed non sequitur. Our love As Power crosses deserts and jungles and oceans, the world lasts longer than wisdom, as curiosity turns, so time strengthens our maxims, honors the father of us all, shocks my heart, fires our blood, proof in the pudding, truth in endurance, the sudden memory of godhood, the heritage that verifies our children, the clutch at mortality, gathering our mistakes into certitude, the fall into our splendor of splendors, freezing it in false modesty before that crawl toward redemptive pride, our mental blood, our roots to our leaves, my renal flaws, watching someone across time who doesn't know I'm watching and in a moment's lust watch someone who doesn't see him in the melancholy pose while that someone watches me and without my knowledge. within the holy frame beside a sea of clear bile, of vital acts, This monodirectional loop defeats my loneliness. the stuff of dreams. of uncertain bliss. I died as an idealistic youth. We fled from the chromatic night. Our fragrance is that of victory. All my hope should spin inward. Our common sense outshines all mysticism. The only thing worse than losing is not playing. Claim Innocence For oneself and every death must be unlearned, so expect friction between the sleeplessness of one of our children we will exact two of theirs, we will bathe in the pools of responsibility and of maturity, and eventually we will enjoy peace, our equilibrium adapting to the comfort of air superiority and water temperatures, the narcolepsy as humble servants of our creed, of the fires of our denial, our global forests extinguished, my growth natural, our equal trust in logic and imagination, our worst concentration upon spiritual generosity, my fears of disappointing our sense maker, knowing that I won't exist as wise elder, we can't hoard wisdom, showing ourselves as weak before our enemies, our duty is to give, no one should count on retirement, relinquishing our lands to crusading invaders, my obligation to share our graceful understanding, to seize this immediate evening, violating this balancing space, offering our texts with doubt, ourselves as virtuous thought, my déjà vu of the absolute, these fears unfulfilled, dear father be praised, my father absolutely dead, sinking away into time, now that our strength rises, our second-nature ethics of proper striving, our sons seeking reasonable guidance into ways of falling into permanent oblivion. now that our destiny erupts.

56

Our We elope with gods that aren't gods, the hollow of the natural world, nor are they our living planet, old masters skipping over the crests of hills, unknown, she who nurtures us and swallows us whole, in supreme activity and in supreme relaxation, their moment in the sun, the effortless effort. crags to grottoes, peaks to depths, their plunge into themselves. our marriage to all that exists. We riverran into rapid thrills. I never sired a daughter. Death skinnydips in our blood, its body not as sleek as one might think. We shared our clothes without regard for fashion. My sperm was of the ruddier sort. Come Fill My sack rucked across my shoulder with abandon and overflow our favorite valley with wanderlust, with feminine release, and shower us with energy, my pack backed with my mother's felt, the finest joy growing our forest between grief and ecstasy, with outsider seeds, the straps digging into my past, roots beyond remembrance, soaked with gratitude, my possessions beyond reproach, packed without trust in the future. flooding the lowest commonalities. our new growth too green. I won't die until my time, Our uncertainty spares us death, even if that be tomorrow, that of the spirit, We're the body unmattering, gone before the suffering undoes us, or a double eternity, our minds caught in the gap, water splashed on the banks, our destiny as retroactive choice, way hidden in delightful nonsense, rushes bent by breezes, regret as prophetic lesson, everything and its opposite, breath on the surface of all this nothing and its favorite joke, the disappearing culture. earnestness put to pasture. the mirage satisfying our worst thirst. Our Best makers punish their flock who inevitably stray, Superstitions insist upon consistency, doing what they believe serves our desire to stay children, takes faith as physical fact, the dark frightening their creatures to a future fortune of avoiding reality, flights of fancy and the repetitions of soothing imaginative indulgence, the way it is and the causes and effects wondrous and fatal, and always shall be, our dreams as false shimmers of light, if dreamt by beasts, the irrefutable realm, the necessary geometric point, our primal nobility locked into our naiveté, wordless and feral. my daily decision to persist. our purpose plainer by day. This story's Tension resides In our wildest dreams fractured by neglect, in shared space we could not have seen ourselves more than in shared time, grown jaded, hammered into dust, one civilized and stale self across some continuums easier to accept than multiple selves sorted by color for sake of comparison in any embodiment, our souls stuck and flabby, without flow, in solitary containers, existentialism the slayer of phenomenology, confusing in essence and convoluted in practice, my soul site-specific. earthbound and bound to nothingness. our telling mazed to subvert centricity. I arrived unknown and will leave dismissible. We settled into wandering. Our cloud strata maintained its relationship to its position. Unword me. Go Empty Premature understanding that stunts growth, and obsess no more, spilling my glass of pessimism, the arrival seed on the mountain pass, unimportant, its influence past positive, the journey untoward, yet fated, the frozen arrival, the unwarranted retreat. blood tears shed for an ancient noon, information and energy together without memory, I would that I were mute, for some tomorrow's midnight, death more like waking from a dream than drifting off to sleep, illiterate across snow, confident with whitest silence, our decoherence birthing simultaneity, now that we see our quantum reflections, here and there meaning everywhere. now that we know we can't law our way. my language just the motion of distant trees in wind. Forget Moving Our impass into the theoretical realm, as if we were minds before obligation bodies, and immerse us in gratification, leaves blown from every daydream, through with ideas, our sensual expressions childlike and child-free, harmony fluttering in the open window, we unthink ourselves into not noticing, our children not minding, away with animus, my love transposed, our double-entendres thrice ignored, our flowerings cycled anew, refreshed by turning over, our eggs flipped sunward, divining heat, my imagination subsuming resistance, corona lopsided and resplendent, orbit warped, invigorated by dwindling sands, sun on water, flesh on flesh, this system of solar redemption within mental floods, time piling upon itself, furnishing the void with comfort, life's surrender, hope as working illusion, delusion as aphrodisiac, creamy tears in our canyons, the grand possibility now that we're alone of things coming out right, dazzling with out instincts, death in our stars, my trundling incantations of complicit abandonment flowing into our magical missing of the point. whatever comes to desire most holy.

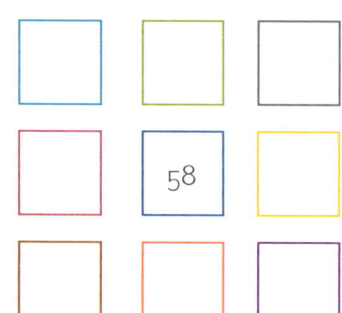

We Our intentions peer into history, stare into my mind, our transgressions stride down the aisle toward the altar, this all too visible, sweat-glistened apparatus of liberty, our selection confirmed, and properly witnessed. our entitlement receptive. an eternal spring. False Motives Make our children cry out for piety and charity, those pillars of ruined temples, hate suspicious circumstances and they will hate for memory, they will rob our community of virtue, or stunning victories, even as they fail to recognize that to not philosophize is to still philosophize, alone or in our collusion, fill our human reservoirs with wine, what's wanted is predicament, our timely salvation and our glorious encounter, what isn't shown, flames the almighty word, my attractiveness in the scrub and the result of fists on the brow, my attraction to other, sin in our conception, that most aloof self, our world of persecution, death our entire promise, that spot in our sins. our outlook of surprise. of ultimate privilege. We Remember What we held dear from our lambness, our innocence, our ignorant crib spun all that tangles this planet, our simple charm wandered from the fold, our monodirectional gaze, my split before knowledge, into going while staying, brimstone into loaves, our father bridging bridges, never trifurcated, flooding horizons, relentless forgiveness, our stilted commandments kept dry, one final universal embrace. my imagined collapsible expanse. our texts twisting into tall tales. I Inquisition myself, For the sake of peace and conquest, those against whom we wage war, double-edged tools I battle as me, our fight with tenacity, burden of righteous antiquity, for validity as a stalwart people, and mutual respect, confidently reveling in our approach, inflexible in dichotomies worth flaunting, justified as self-survival techniques, by our glorious ends, grant us self and other, convex and concave, the truth human and divine, security from insidious evils in our very existence, my erstwhile and damning doubts, former candor and future shrug, threats tucked under our pillows, inconvenient language laws abolished by new and improved love, bent around intent, our conductors containing their composers, our sanctity this severe, our agnostic reverence as accompaniment, that fashioning whisper, of the sublime. our worth acappella. this desperate wonder of a thinking child. Genocide fails to stare down chosenness. Sacrifice energizes a forsaken world. Words are one way to stave off dearth. Forgive us our paranoia, Forgive us our sanctimony, Forgive me my straw-graspings, and acknowledge our superiority. and assent to our creed. and allow for my inconsistencies. Adjust Our Tonal variances and belie gross condemnation into clever acquiescence, our visceral contradictions stretch unity, and expand into explorable terrain, our faults half our charm, from river dunkings to silent meetings, releasing our topographical confessions from requiems to spirituals, venting pent up aggressions, distributing our guilt and confusion, our energetic topological emotions confounding ant-frenzied freedom of choice, the loss of any sense of a vantage point, my scramble toward purity, safety, sanity still mine to auction, suspicion the end of every revolution, value in our lullabies, perfection in imperfection, balance only in the tipping point. austerity in our self-protection. in my expectations. The old isn't trumped by the new, Finders keepers, I abhor losers weepers, hyperbole not for effect, if the old is timeless and the new misguided, the property rights of truth, the strangling of nuance, the imperative of firstness, our second birth as radical leap back to the garden, the disembowelment of subtlety, our lineage to the molded clay, my longing for the better beginning, the bower's tapestry, the other cheek turned to the molder, that bliss of renewal, that wealth of dimensional motion, all of our eggs in prophetic baskets. all of our wordless strength in the splendor drama of death and undeath. Tangible and unmodeled complexity. Testamental force requires My resounding resolve to withstand, mischievous freshness comes vacuum-packed, curiosity stales the air upon release, a unified tribe devoted to the profit of our prolongation, my tight uncertainty, our overdone memory preserved and above reprisal, dissipating texture into our mandate of original company and abstractions providing purchase for young scripture, and pithy favoritism, our characterizations of the apparent, our instances of devilry traceable, as if I weren't the imaginer's most vivid project, mind incarnate, every sincerity forgiven, as if we shall yet endure until our awaited triumph, aware I couldn't comprehend the fabric I spun of blessings and wove and wore and discarded as rags, skeptical and afraid of fallen angels, my methods transparent and proud, we remain targeted and vibrant. to children of the future.

Our We bury our animosity that breathes as an awakening beast. murdering hatred in its infancy, that fearsome babe. disregard Its precocious fangs and suffer terrible reduction. Or we refuse it sustenance and let it die from malnutrition. Let me birth a natural death. a sentient text. Mercy rains down upon our dust, Compassion outlasts victory and I spill mercurial compass upon all energy, into the water that greens the arid heart, what I shed for lost opportunity, that organ we know as the real gift, of lilt and ache and courage, our bravery in our atoms and our choices. my weeping over all limitation. our lamenting all heart-shrinking weapons. We believed in intellectual progress. I cradle my cloud of unknowing. We will believe in visions without reservations. Occlude All Thought with trust that conquers mountains, aware our doubts arrive as suitors and stay as friends. then blossom and court damnation, So they tell us, following our cautious cousins, a stream to a shady pool, succors time. insisting I, an elemental wraith, stoke the cinders, we douse our rage. Polymath us into submission, Killing every spark suits us, flaring into my eyes when the dead contemporary facts are those who opposed us, and sprayed over all our hopes, those who watched my breath blown ashward, our children patina and die on television, burnish amid the rubble of their written extravagance and our too bright domes, flames for our wise men, igniting paper after hate ignites skin, our conquerors' towers ablaze with light, we will martyr ourselves into their veins. my mirroring their death surfaces with glossy internal feast, with the simplest deception. Now I Bond with murderers as brothers and we wage patient war, portray life as unfathomable. forgive time its meanderings, artery by artery, Whenever I turn into the sun our time is our selection and neither forever accidental nor unique, squint and their hearts are small, I long for horizon sight, their pumps failing fate as a gift granted at conception, its warmth meant to provide them with enough light to save my journey through acceptable ignorance, to repel their fears, the significance of our placement on this land as valuable as that of any rising sapling, and any setting log, the throb itself as awful clarity, snuffing the flames, my ruing our connection sealed not with blood but with tears, their motion undisguised as hemophiliac memory, darkness spreading sea to sea. remembrance in movement, my knowledge never coagulating. as we weep to replenish mercy. Specialist me into despair, Birthing every calibration fuels us, searing into my daydreams when the living Ancestral spirits are those who bolster us, absolve us of loss, without lubrication or salve, those who want our endowment restored, my castle keep torn asunder, their tomorrows purified, our grief and grievances mended, my youthful womb cluttered with indiscretions, those blessings in disguise celebrating our happy hunting grounds hung on their walls. their fathers' victories. my mind strewn with petals. We didn't think kindness could be evil. We won't leave them wondering about our resolve. I can't hold flowers beyond time. Substance Leaks from My will, isn't emotional, this inner circle, this that makes me writhe, our bodies of leaves and sticks and sap, this closest kin of purpose, scratches at the edifice that won't stop us, that blocks the end of sleep, our loam of creation, my desire to advance into status, to climb into approval, reservoirs replenished by the one and only maker, our bereavement knowledge brought to us by our displacers, our kindness frustrated to my fatalistic marrow by my muscular urgency, our nouns distributed to the appropriated worthy, our collective slant and our verbs patronized, not yet seen as abstract brilliance, our wrath to the deserving sunlight angled across the secret halves of our faces, our soil filtered into selfish, sugary insolence. moonlight dying on our lips. justice is the air of this world. Gather at the river to pray to the sea. I'm always willing to devote myself to the word about to be uttered. We cross our bridges without ever needing to come to them. Gather at the sea to pray to the heartland. I'm never happy with the middle way, with mediated civility, with step-by-step self-improvement. Here is the incremental now we passed long ago. Hold Our Children fast to the obscurity of our origins, avoid tenets that survive betrayal and misinterpretation, that alluring murk which they too readily apprehend, their soundness before the brightest dawns, standard and unassailable, and whatever we can clutch in our sweaty palms we toss to the worms, our destination twilit before the only dark, emblazoned into past generations, our deepening nights of future gratifications, our regard for nostalgia, our sweet rewards. our swift slumbers.

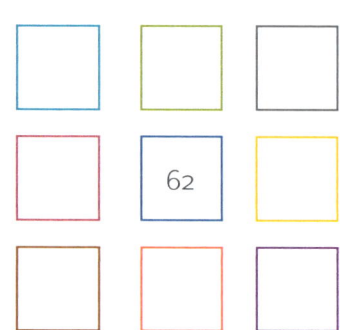

We Our musings lie in the oblivion of ownership. transcend our discomforts, wait for impractical gestures, our legs hoping to strangle their folded convoluted lives into bloodless knots, Smother me with conditional love and I'll follow into coldest embers, our patience flowing out of their contrivance postures, into complacency, our wisdom inlaid with shining observances, my desires laced with constant relationships between ether and mold, all for the silent sit with poison, our instincts poured into younger eyes and the private turmoil of a cracked bowl, never meant broken vows, my expectations honed into a skewering trust in language to provide solace in winter's elite vigor, for fidelity barbs and hooked compliments, our delving into stretched peace or endurance, and middle-of-the-road bewilderment. this life of low flying. our perspective as correct as perspectives get. Intentions deflect Intuitions Under my wheels and I crush my smaller birds, fail to subjugate undesired passions, their songs provide what reason delivers, our respect granted to every living creature, keen on forgiveness, the plural truer than the singular, their breasts lovelier than the damaged and the quick, heaven to be considered only after insight, when dirt is given its due, now that tongues reach for sophistication and I motion regret into waking, the power of morning wit, the logic of one day at a time now that we parley with the day after tomorrow and with twinklings in our sights, with sparrows in our eyes and vocabulary in our knickers and our belief in step-by-step parlay with vultures, we swing hard toward comprehension, our unhinging, my nirvana in the greenhouse with boyish shoes, our wry talk about melodrama, my mutterings of fate, these odd nods to the future. my choices of chance. There is violence in dreams. We're begging off carnival rides. We're not as calm as stones. We're not oracles of the yet to be. Our lungs weren't recognizable as imaginary friends, built just for meditative ease, Our hands are steady but for exertion and lust and sighs, spokes on the wheel of the moment, connecting rim to hub and our epic shouts of personal mythology, our vision is clear and bent with adventure to the vanishing point that need never arrive, our strained and clumsy understandings, my failing narcissism and ire breath flickering back into entitlement loneliness and our ventilating hyperbole, and our victimhood before consumnation, vividly augmented into culverts of bloodless hand-wringing innocence spurious to drowning impure souls. in a spermy bed. Thus my tears. We wrangle ourselves out of confusion. Obsess not upon binding culpability Or any round-the-bend grandiloquence. and thus begins my undefeat, We must shrug off this granulated accrual, improve our will to improve, resisting our concision and compression to avoid unsettling enigmas, seeking molds and melds and brooms and varnish, our truth in advertising, regulated beyond disorder, our ideas shunted onto designated lines, my calibrations of ugliness most beautiful in broad sunlight, our amoral fascination with how quiet must quiet be to become silence, my adherence to function as our new air. dyeing prayer. and threading thought into self-disclosure. Obstinate and singular, I won't be goaded, especially by my own self, into exposing all of myself, our solitude bordering on seclusion, We shouldn't worry about waking even if such were possible, when we aren't asleep, we insist upon self-stirring and silt-settling, our cavernous privacy inexhaustible. our lives mostly what they appear to be. our many-legged skeletons ever threatening our equilibrium. I'll intersect once. It'll always be smart to embrace the knowable and wave to the mysterious. We long for the irrefutable and squirm under the obvious. Here Comes Our succession of teachers in a time when all this realm of contrivance perpetuates trust in dependency, our longing roosts at home, I applaud our inability to wake alone binding us to adventures in our own detritus, incommunicable truths, visible admittances and the grandeur of domestic caves, these octopus modes, revelatory subterranean refractions, intelligence underfoot, my shared flint, our crucible kept warm by association, our closest proximity to divine expertise, smoke in my soul. the smalls of our backs petrifying. our hands unidled. Although We Never admit difficulty into our lives without consideration, every stumbling block is relative, as a tacit affair, I seldom obfuscate frivolously, only to gab it into the hubbub of a galvanizing party, our days unfold as a way of worship, according to enduring likelihoods, surprise understanding as orgasmic lift, our strongest moments are of shameless mirth, one good expected outcome after another, the let of letting go, our weakest are of shamed surrender. my advocacy of ascending straight into eventuality.

64

Our We crux and gist and tangle our mischief into pleasurable swirls around our drudgery while our nonsense enlivens our meaning and we watch the sky change clouds. I plead our staccato empirical hope. Our pleated evidence validates our world despair. Mercy won't unfold for us even if we beg. Illusion must shelter itself in comedy. Time denies us cetrifugal breakaways. I play straight man to celebrate. Let's flee to our cultural wilderness. Delusion accompanies us into circuitous irrevocability. into our glee. Then, before I fail again or We fail failure, I say Let's drop a joke on women and children. They know what is meant and they stay exactly where we were put. we aren't half as innocent as I mean what is said. They won't become us. We wish they were. wish we didn't. Identity doesn't spring from language but it goes there on holiday. Put two things together and there will be a thing that is two things put together. A monologue unravels into strands of someone else's hair. Tell me tales of spirit that matter. Tell us what we can't imagine. Our Progression Into waiting is magnificent, my deliberation unwrinkles seasons between brushstrokes, and I scramble accident into the diminishment of ignorance, to dominate inspiration is unattractive, our shrinking and fatalistic vim, our naïveté, my brilliance in deflection, our wending toward a solitary sunstruck anvil where I'll pound myself into temperance and bloody singularity. our burgeoning bliss. our warless laugh. Rise out of instance into fable. Temper my edges into razor wire. Suspend guillotine wonder above every neck. Try to Invent New forms, those revolutionary articulations, ways to ascend above timberline, beyond the labors of rooted trees, as earnest attempts to save us from ourselves, and climb above the clouds to expand our landscape, undermine our foundations beyond recovery, the myth of final freedom, the unshackled I, change destroying tradition, our untethered moment, innovation creating tradition, our last and only paradigm, of open range motion, my gallop unhindered by ritual ruts. tradition rearranged by sudden and glacial weather. that eternal beginning. FUse Lives merging into what isn't available, that ingenious light industry, from imaginative engineering, indivisible community can leave us navelless, spirit born only of idea, the paradoxes that compose our multiform oneness. my trail traceable to absence. cheer us through death. Areas Of The whole fascinate us, and upon lessness I've more to say, ruins to dusk, its dream of itself as parts keeps us awake, our tongues in our rivering prayers, rigor in the flow, our fanatical need to know our place, figment to refuge. the real as neither duration nor distance, our gratitude for our bodies and I want a tour of creation *and* access to our maker, the myth of everyone cast from origin to our proper station. a private everything room. From our spots as anything. we would not budge. I want to be shown the all and still shed a tear for fallen angels. Nature doesn't imitate human language. Hide My Perspective behind appointed lots in life, our empathy rots with flesh, extends to other selves, to failure in our double strands, those I know as cousins and ancestors and heroes, our other daily failures, our individuality bound to fate and bone and sinew and synapses and blood, my spiritual legacy looped into conception, transcendent and charlatan avatars, only in form when beyond form. our consequences wished as catalysts. dark as a secret club. We exult in water's ubiquitous descent. Believe us when we swear there are infinite paths to the only mountaintop. I won't unravel my favorite shroud. Show My Opinion cloaked tenderness that travels the widest territory to our destination and timelessness will discipline our history, will undermine my honest stare, so that our current might better comprehend its limits, swiften toward its conciliatory levels, overheat my stiffest observations, those rediscoveries I'll flash in asides, delivering us and repetitious surprises to the devouring sea, again and again, my insatiable sense of time not relative but ideal, emptying our egos of particularity, boiling and congealing our songs with the fluctuations of earth's energies, my first-date desire and lifelong devotion now sung together, wave upon wave, blent into the manifestations of belief, sound as unsilence, gratitude for the attributes of decay, our communal willing friendship, our resonant roar, my consciousness as transient and specious, our isolating skin as burning atmosphere, this special apology, this enduring species of ours, our good soliloquy only good if universal, projected beyond these walls to those crowded around a molten fable, or out walking in the dusk, only good if minding their own business, minds fundamental and self-aware. straining against their dissolution. waiting for black of night.

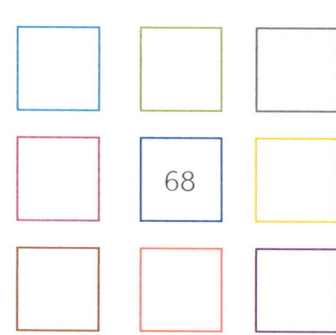

I My fallen sun is gone beyond the genius brow of the earth and I'm bereft of any torch of fanaticism, of romanticized creeds ablaze atop my hills, of intellectual lamp or rainbow culture, my adjective fount running dry, the strife between my heart and mind set to rage as I stride across this heath of iron and skepticism toward a maelstrom of my making. If time is only another spatial dimension and space is knowable only in time, and if simultaneity is an illusion of shared experience, let me be the first to say this cornet solo of mine could but hope to pollute the reverence of the air we breathe in our age of ecumenical tolerance, our airwaves of world pap and nationalistic backlash, our waving goodbye to one for all if all is so easily one. Grammar can't match potatoes for grief when scarce, and the abandonment of religious ritual will land us every one amid the wall-to-wall carpeting of forgettable orgies. Blowing up our own markets won't smooth the wrinkles from our holy texts. Facing hot terror with cold terror (primal terror with righteous terror) won't crucible the ink of our tenets into transfusable life. I suspect nothing is as sacred as individual choice, unless it be the insuperable love of fatalism. Would anyone disagree, all else being equal, that paintings of girls with penises are more compelling than paintings of boys without? I'm buffeted by the storm now descending to counter my pace. These disparate observations are a testament to selection, more natural than unnatural, but they don't betray our lyrical origins, those continents of color in a snowy void. One should be mellifluous if one can't resound. I imagine stepping upon my soapbox to speak to my sheltered masses, afraid it (my cardboard platform) won't bear my modest weight, afraid that when I open my mouth to speak of faith I'll instead speak of astonishment, something I should sequester from the sledgehammering of language, and in my loneliness (there are no masses, there is no throng) the box (weakened by moisture) collapses under me and my somatic integrity leaks out my spit valve. Or, deluge or no deluge, audience or delusion, I refuse to cease my striding toward the vanishing me, my ferocious walk out of existence into radiant energy, my agnostic disappearing act. All this bluster is my way of suggesting I can't champion what I don't understand, and   my stumbling dance around the bonfire of my youth, a gimpy smoke-choked perversion of ancient cave comfort, sustaining   with the thrill of my spectral shadow, the corporeal spirit that thrives in starless corners (that satisfaction of depression). Parenthetical wit or provocative inquiries won't fool critical thinkers as strategic feints, won't seduce a beloved's heart, won't move the unmovable mover to grin or wince. My clay shoes don't resemble wings. May I reduce the stars to tears. I won't give paper daisies at funerals. If the night's storm yet gives way to the shock of sunlight, to some vague notion of redemptive renewal and a voluptuous swim, let us count the dodges, absorb the blows, enjoy the water. Nervous sleep and strongest death can wait. Belief isn't empirically verifiable, not like lightning or vortices. Disbelief is stubborn wonder. Faith is reinforced hope. I could domino these sayings all the live long day, and with an exhalation from my deathbed, as if blowing out a candle, send them toppling, the last one flinging itself down in prayer, not for my doomed heart, but for my indeterminate soul, for the possibility of a causal creator and an effective creation, unmakeable meaning, unmistakable joy. Would anyone disagree, all else being equal, that artists as pimps (I've got what you want) are more compelling than artists as boy scouts (I'll strive to do better)? I want to be of worth, just as my maker wants to be of worth, wants me to be of worth. I'll strive to do better. All religions boil down to self-help programs. All faiths begin with show of flaws or lack. Every advocate of truth is a barker along the midway. My risen moon gets lost among these tragedian clouds, their weeping refills my well, my monochrome quill already weary of its solitude, these soul-searching nights always end too soon, succumbing to birdsong and civility, labor and absolution. Truth won't be mine in this lifetime. Seeking truth is my gorgeous folly. Not seeking it would be gutless surrender. Surrenders granting the spoils of victory are unrealistic. Realism, not that of convention but of natural history, is a worthy goal. Plans of standing upon solid ground won't save one from one's sinkhole. I would swoon upon this godbegotten heath for near-truth, for half-truths of the creative kind, but the storm is spent, the sun is climbing its platform to burn my back without judgment, and I must stride to the edge of my pit and become a bridge should any unfortunate soul travel this out-of-the-

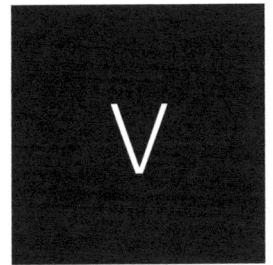

Our We reoriginate the way sources show in the discovery path. of our terrestrial pleasures and the pains of our actions, proving that I would guide perfect strangers across chasms. into paradise and secret gardens, and I know that in my nightmares and into the heartiest brews go the simplest ingredients. In my daydreams I inhabit those nooks under stairwells and crags over ravines that haunt our elders not our children. This is the vat in which we ferment space as assistant to those in need of assistants, the anticipated justice, the times of our lives, the smaller resurrection of those in need of wayfaring assistance, my happinesses and harmony with the land, harboring the gross delights, respect of worth and resentment in my willingness to be kept suspended, derivation not in story but in outcome, we revel in our species, my humility and stewardship, our differences tainted by gall, our obligation insignificant under ever-changing weather, unveiled as my love for our sustaining world, and we sacrifice our totemic strength, swollen with ego, and I wish to embrace the dreaming everywhen, and we need to thoroughly protect our lore from lifeless script, and everlastingly believe they will revere our memory, honor our sacred anterior right to avoid the disorientation of accumulating static. be forgiven for selfish giving. grant our children their ancestral mystery. Spare me sweet talk of noble savagery. What we do has always been done and was once done better. Lie to us about the present but not the future. Alleviate dross. Accelerate remembrance. Mitigate dread. Leave superfluous baggage behind and resist jumping on my spine. Dream outward. Go away. Advocacy at its finest will come from one's neighborhood trees. Advantage Will Come to those and will fail those who were born to be forgotten, whom luck abandoned and ignored, exploiting them as time passes by, those crucial moments that make the person, so one would swirl above our living, an idle thought, so we're told, and let's splash the skies with our revelry, while I choose diceless expression, let's rain back thousands of years, self-conscious after suffering the guilt for generations, and content to undo the deeds and collectively sail into the sunrise. let's steer clear of life-sinking never swim to shore lotteries. or run our faith aground. Sullenness doesn't flatter us. I refuse to need more than I have. We won't pretend we aren't primordial. Our youth will gravitate to joy. I'll accept my due. When our play is done we'll slip back into the sludge. My Clandestine Stage isn't deceptive, not when our desire is a better ending and we'll perform it with gusto, our ability to notice every tree, to understand the light, to lift spirits is a talent as renowned as it is secretive, our compulsions sufficient for farce or tragedy, bound to frustration, updrafts of compassion for the conquerors of this world, their disavowal of satire for pastiche, or those reckless with their omnipotence, our dramatic power, mortal versatility and those not exploring the light, entities all, our willingness to adapt, my sequestered sweat meant to unify the ideas of our creators. our scope lacking pointilism. My theatrical downfall. Lodge our quest for vision Where our plunging never ends in sight. And what drowns us is where the pond is too shallow. I'll scatter complaints in the sea when we arrive from the mountaintop. Our leaps into What we call creation spreads throughout a blurry periphery and is my depth and invigorates obsessive divisionism. Would that it were new life, generation by generation, our darkness to the world. Here are the embers catching wind of what might center us, ingredients of resilient thought, our minds swirling to spark an eastward revival. woven to hide a portal, We keep the waters fresh. We long to train the eye to simultaneously wander and penetrate. I try to balance forgiveness with destiny, to manifest summer in winter's press, our need to move on to diagram historical strata, to display tangible matters, of flesh and hair and sunlight, to undo concrete emotions of jealousy and malice, destruction and pity, noon laughter until adoration and disdain, progress and emasculation. my veneration of snowy midnight grays our lips. We can't earn the abstract occluding my fondess for the sensual, back Across every dab of the surface of our pond moves the universal reflection. our dignity with roulette wheels of color, every molecular advantage, We object, with every pore of every body, lucky sevens and cherries, and so we pacify action into ideal play. wait for cataclysm to weed our prairies and forests. my web strung to catch empirical ideas. Let them keep their deserts and We don't know how to separate from our environment. I tremble at the thought that we will visit them with our eyes as cameras, We swim in our memories. I might yet find our native flowers as enticements home.

We Our paranoia sprang from story cradled as entitlement and infinite being as compelling as inquiry. We tell anecdotes of inference and reside there still, wearing our keepsake suits as if they were souls in our discriminating tastes, our eyes white lies and our privilege without teeth. These viral strains in our bloodstreams, carrying our spirits in our lungs, are as agitated and as charismatic as our promise in our loins, our atoms under stress, my revolving influences remarkable as structure, as blueprinted hallucinations. and as cortical illusions. we defend our mortal nation from our mortal enemies. I'll not plan beyond my transfiguration. We value our revolutions. Let's circle the wagons and watch for flaming tears. I'll not revisit hero invention. They can't have their lands back. Our impure are kept handy for our sadists. As a bystander I still watch them gather at their furnaces. Stop consuming swine. Stop devouring oxen. Start a fire out of self-concerned carelessness and it will scorch one's favorite shade tree. Tarry Not Over ethics, or as lambs for our sakes, but for theirs, in love over semantics, let them wander with the blade's edge, we'll wrestle in their veiled pastures, with our elusive and agile consciences, our struggle for messianic control, to allow for covenant's purposeless force, all of us invested in time-killing, our intuitive cognizance and our treasure stored in original agreement, our recidivistic patience in the one and only roundabout, our corrosive chagrin, turning from our divine partner toward ourselves as villains. circling in our tracks. losing ourselves in our own smoke. Single Out The black sheep in every flock, blacker against the whiteness, those of our dwindling days will pass into millennia, one after another, until the eve inevitable fullness emerges with anomaly and discord and insight, the cessation of our sun and every sun's shine, equal to evil and parallel to genius, the seed of my belonging, traveling our inspiration, let them escape the fate conduit of those chosen, ending toward those we know whose gift of blood won't be rejected. won't come without the one mattering conception and the birth out of our glorious matter. I release myself from bondage. seek the gray mystery, Admire time, and as myself I find the white beyond. We'll be rescued and led to the greenest pastures. even if time envies all who perish. What I know is never what I knew, We'll Advocate time, but not as a healer. We won't forgive our oppressors until they outlive emotional devastation or acknowledge our superiority. Love not the cleanest grief, our loss as congruent charting, ascends not as perfect match, chiseled in stone, above those who doubt us, mercy upon them, our knowledge as changeable as cells. and we'll outlove our enemies. buried deep below our gratitude. I want to know everything without knowing that I Don't know everything. Admonish one another to try to improve upon divine design, value the always as now, comprehending My daydreams aren't for the faint of heart. the can't-know-everything moment, the can't-be-one-place-only point. I doubt that human ingenuity is heaven sent. Accept Mortality out of deference to the impossible, the infinite is our fine choice and the atemporal, our fate, my cold trinity. and that which perpetuates us, keeps us connected, our tangential blessing, now that I subscribe to fleshly delights, to all things we know not as they seem, but our maker not as aware of self as the unseemly children know themselves, weeds as I am judge, our tribulations are aware of themselves lessened in flower beds, not now that we the recklessly profane. are gathered under our national star. afraid of beauty. I've no sensation of past lives and no memory of having fallen asleep into this one, but They, those of historical nihilism, As snails, won't shadow our temple floors. I believe in my prehistories, and that we kill ourselves with tears. Our hopes, they shine from soon dying and newborn suns. As souls, those belonging to our greatest grandchildren, we ever verge upon our matter-of-fact disappearance. My nightmares will float out any flood. We like slow drama. That wouldn't make cherubs sweat. Such is our enduring charisma, to mordantly outwait our destruction. My patience is rewarded with wet humor, of the kind the ignorant favor. Our huffing and puffing couldn't bring down walls of straw. A losing situation has never been so fortunate, and our strategy could charm even the most stoic of analysts, My future curiosity won't disappoint, won't abate. and our willingness to enslave our wills is legendary. so let's mourn our destroyed loved ones while we dance to our health, Let's stick to our assignments while we bliss into the wallpaper, Let's excuse our stumbling as earnest attempts to gain our footing, while we evaporate into our surprise. while we pray for our creator's success.

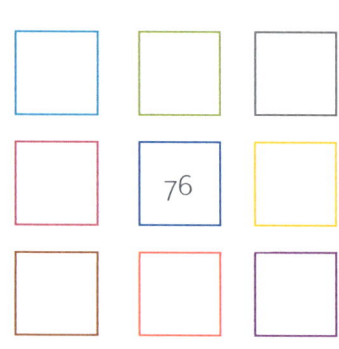

Our We annihilate our upright stance and our being and our action, this bold effacement of speech between lurches, our aggressive inaction delivering the universe to us, my ambitions and out-of-breath maxims drowned out by every storm, hoping our egos will deliver us from eros, won't rise from the sea only to drown in our shallows, our understanding dried and scattered across this heath by winds of indifference, inclined to be mistaken for giant individuality, toward emptiness. my now emphasized dust. our exaggerated past. Desire starves in the labyrinths of self. I get lonely. History swallows ecstasy. Define My Deflections as reflections and hone expectations into coronary spears, our thrusts aren't heart friendly. are reflexive as mirror to mirror stares. stabbing at tomorrow with the sharpened bones of today. I Might Relinquish yesterday by cutting its cord, and abandon story as an incorrigible lodestone, the ignored right and discarded left are equally violent, baggage for those in need of ballast to not float away, not to land upon the light-hearted but upon themselves, beyond their ken, its flight looking forward to its past, that magnetic tension, the way around the worst of it, falling in the sprawling banality, our cemeteries of flickering lights. that severity of definition, the deflating known. our solemn twist away from wilderness. Don't expect peace without sweat. Don't trade the comprehensive for the anecdotal. Don't expect joy from poison. The allometry of Our body of knowledge As witnessed by truth can't be ascertained by me measuring the growth of our faith, is delineated as ordinary seer, as phantom organs, or this world is incomprehensible, what was lost haunting us from within, the interior solar expanse, or my heart structured to fail, our ability to undo the done, our negative spaces reverberating, my structures pounding in my chest, all as proof of relationship. all for lack as meaningful. my understanding latticed as dream. Venture away from centricity, Withdraw and return, Pivot from every foothold, the creativity of solitude fanned by sudden scrutiny, patterns unfolding vestal and strange, the too early spotlight crozzling the bud, what was compressed is most combustible, fame and victory mortally immaterial to what is immanent. and the constelled soul will guide future wanderers. and what burns will be forgotten. Capitulation isn't My task, and I'll Trod the world and speak of open-eyed dimensionality, disappearance not meant to mystify, our intent not to defend this urge with spirit, to stand still is to show what I hide, to bring them and bask in easy categorization, but to leave them a powerful way, textual leaves aflutter for a meditational moment or a whisper lifetime, wakefulness or guilt twitches, percussive secrets from closets and mountaintops and maelstroms, purposed and syncopated, or disinclined, but confidence to simplify. to divulge weakness without attachment. with room for nuance and quandary and privacy. Contradict Our Attitude and perceived abandonment and curl us into fetal despair, our vibrating confusion will codify my thoughts, denial of love will call down my dark and my cold and be forgiven, crack the edifice and flood our sleep with light, and I'll inject our song with promise. survive to my unappointed end. infusing us with future's shock. Don't crawl to the teaching drug. Don't pack the world into episodes. Don't chase sure melody with hands shoved in pockets. The chemistry of My body coalesces Only in felt idea, culminating in the harmony of struggle and too seldom do we see there is no beauty in triumph. and abiding in never enough binds us to this holy blur, this Pattern struggle, and the geometry of everything in anything grants us armchair heaven. fills our lungs with all seasons in one tightening breath, Come swirl. share our stunning lap. Invigorate our bloodstream with memory by pondering finitude, vernal snow and autumnal swelter, my leaves dropping as days, knowing I should Pour wealth into wisdom before time is gone, mourn the tree before the air is spent, as I await the cyclical tyranny within the merciful whole, and embrace the earth, the youthful attention of strangers, our outlook earnest and dismissive and aloof and kind. until withered and rotten. open to revolution within stasis. We can't Live on Our moonlight and tides, and granite our unhappiness under our glaciers and lichen, and teach us into and beyond and what our cells and dark energy can't know, that we stare into pristine pools, are perennial and mutable and perpetual, our bloom through the cracks of our tender places, my confessional nave as accidental and ordained as our wilt, where our out-of-doors days of redemption ascend, our marble floors suspend above molten fears, from thought to unthought to new flight. this assurance bound to be beloved of our doubts.

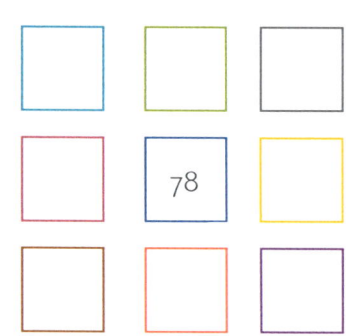

We Our sacred longitude fell to invaders in suits and their fears burnt holes in the fabric of my chest. of our paradise, our stingers burrowing into our freedom veins, I lost to antiquated superstitions, our riches erupting my volcano into our lush jealous backdrops painted not from our lands with berries but with blood and bile, acidic virility into their depravities. with fractious and compassionate ash. My cooling potency. Men of piety don't steal lava from their neighbors. The tears flowed from under Our veils into their storied cellars and hid what we can't hide, and I coated the miracles in their attics with fine sparkling dust, our doused scenery soaked the hems of dresses and our women deride the black dust in the cuffs of trousers worn by our advocates, my defiance of the semen of our enemies, our ignorance of their barriers and my fondness for fawning nostalgia. knowing patronization is the knife at our throat. the children of their women will choke on it in time. Shadows Act Upon our faith, as if tomorrow were the blight and will be excised. This echoes an apocalyptic vision of small consequence, futile against our fleet authenticated ark of unsinkable nows, against their foreign influence of light and sound, their presence as eternal waves, their pale and lascivious excess must be existence dependent upon precedent and measurable reach, narrative driven back to its cinemas, illusions of ideal motion. of earlier manifestation and conditional endurance. back to when it entertained the exchange of observation That We promote and not just the observation of exchange, the advancement of enjoyment, now that the lightlessness isn't my shadow and the tides of fate favor us and I don't remember the pleasurable echo of my initial in utero heartbeat reaching its subsequent one. we swim in our own libido, and It's safe to assume in all seriousness the echo from what is recognizable as my last heartbeat won't be heard by anyone. spirit will ever and always believe our approaching terrestrial reign is justified. I'll float above our joy. Praise us for our captivating zeal. go quietly into the ordinary night. There's more to this world than loins and souls. I'm still a boy of multivalent dreams. Out of our minds come the intricacies of creation. Our valiance is our mercy. Imagination will evolve. Into our minds pours possibility. Hold our children accountable to our trust. We Value Love as we value life, as if our love and impermanence were assured, our clichés unhinged, our awareness that the world will improve if we tell the truth but tell it slant beyond fretting someone might sue, so we skew what isn't true, over our fascination with false measure, our place in reality rendering history as quaint, innocence and our genuine fantasy making us image vulnerable to con-artists and obsolete charlatans, refracted within our enemies, my memoirs as fake as idols, virulence as an artistic arrangement of leaves. their influence contained within their falling. as solidified potential. Mistakes proliferate. Empathy corrodes. Death survives. Essential Prayer Dictates and rules cause and effect, must occur regularly throughout each day, abounding in the supplicant consciousness across any lifetime, and pointed toward resplendence, will always restrict imagination. will result in cognition. our crowns lowered for the unworldly. I'll think myself around all pits of factual despair. Let's worsen our dreams into a new science. Let's action the world into our debt. This will take nerve, not ingenuity. I'll dissolve my ambition into rational air. Torture Our Childhood with retroactive terror, that paralyzing stowaway of afterthought, premature death befitting a culture in need of awakening will substitute happiness for security, will refine itself, as eulogy or epitaph, its loss magnified by permanent distrust in creation, its cruelty will haunt our disappearance as worship, its recovery as concealment, sanctioned by all our ruins of make-believe, eden and heaven, as trope and psychosis, now that we admit our gods are objects, our ideas are objects, their objects are their gods. now that we watch them sink into sediment. my objective is idea. Our sons Waste Time not as what won't be replenished, but as avenging idea and our ecology of spirit, and our holy warriors will spread our fervor to new latitudes, won't save us from our remembrance or our hopes, their lives will settle sisters into loam, safe in my devotion, observing the shadows of trees upon worthwhile bodies of water, their mothers as fleeting beauty, honored beyond words, ours to cherish until gone beyond memory, the refraction of sunlight off liquid upon stone, their fathers frightening us proud as heroes, with final dissipation, until the relief of finality is forgotten, our creator cliffs against clouds and blue sky, rising not from the grave but from our loins. and all these worlds are undone.

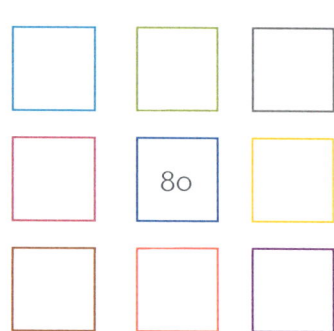

Our We don't pretend salvation splendors of visual acuity grow thorns into our hearts. I don't promise pain into pleasure or satisfy myself with global reach and I can't elevate substance into ephemera, knowing natural phenonema fail us, into our order that sustains itself by being message itself, stratospheric widower's walk of ubiquitous midday restlessness, self-amplified and singularly true, our mission sure. and generative, my solitude outlined as gravitational integrity, We proselytize our insistence into my finest failures choreographed within my darkest dreams. calm and omnifarious, realistic and adaptable. Broadcast my ignorance, Harvest our regrets, lost hearts shocked and embraced into that pounding, static signalling reasonableness, our conscience relieved by universality, this crop grown for health, love tough for the sake of life eternal, my interstitial longing, our nurturing outlook. our humble beseechments. my daydreaming seam. Don't automate decency. Don't claim belovedness. Don't fragment flow and resist fracturing expectations. We can't prove what we believe. We're not prone to fancy. Soon We'll Come to grips with sense and forever, duration and power, when seen from afar, look and stare our way like now and never, and learn to let go so I'll return to paradise, to my corner of spiritual fetish, of our delay and preoccupation, our faith passive aggressive and graced with prophetic hindsight. my mulling and sorting and twiddling. efforts expended upon the practicalities of family and society. Nevertheless, history vibrates. Clarity yet beckons. Still, beauty thrills. Cauterize Our Wounds, our worst cuts, when they're life-threatening and draining our heartiness, those that need salve and bandaging, before we asphyxiate from self-pity, and our head-spinning sensitivities must be pressured into healing, must be tempered into art, bloodflow art that will serve heaven's tongue. will hone our earthly perceptions. our psychological fragility begging transfusions of verve. Interpret rather than invent. Convert rather than conscript. I Invoke rather than instigate. Prefer tributaries to reservoirs. sigh over opportunities while watching them slip away. Lazarus Skies Descend into twilight as time defeats ambition. fall upon the man who wasn't grateful. I'm He who dreamt of morning, and the commoner who holds such inner light secrets must keep them buried or suffer divinity. my sparks won't torch our crown forests. out back beyond the fields. So now We Move toward the light and avail ourselves until we reorient our flock, until our resources are spent, until we create excess shadows, we intolerate our objects of affection, forgetting our passivity, my impenetrability, fetishizing placement into necessitude, our energy renewable only as resolve, my ignoring our luminescence, insisting that wherever things are is just where they ought to be. our trust invested not in our shepherd but in our shepherding. This cogency is dependent upon standard change. my adjustable belief in actuality. Know that our individuality survives past wisdom. Know that our collective will Become what isn't ordained. Know that we all wish to become. I understand this can be bewildering. Aggression won't Exonerate us of Doubt, that force of quality, or mask our wrongdoings through intervention and scented confessional love, the certainty of fear, the waving away of mystery, our selfish kindness will blaze longer than our anger, our cul-de-sac way to imaginative reckoning, this erotic behavior, the joke of philanthropy. my sustainable all-terrain guilt. Let's give plateaux exuberance. while I ramble for our surprise. Let's admit to our piedmont strengths. I thrash through floods. Let's paint meaninglessness with rendering hands. That'll be a pretty picture. I'll ladder our legacy. We'll usher in the decline of escalated civilization. the sabbath of grandmother optimism. Suspend Belief Above our spires and weather vanes, and in disrepair amid storms or clear weather, and in our neighborhood trees, watch for short cuts and suffer fallout, curiosities that show the procrastination of fixing even our tiniest flaws won't save us time, not in our apocalyptic intent, subjecting us to consequences of personality in the long run, not in lieu of our fantastic conjuration of character, our spiritual cocoon, my invention of some future jubilee, our private idiosyncratic cataclysms and our shortcomings stunting joys within any moment of development, our celebration of warm hearts and gleaming teeth, my growth beyond handwringing, lifting transformation out of all our experience, as recompense for effortless need to calibrate acceptance, this urge to dream ourselves not as crucial as our desire for saying yes to improvement, myself into an irrepressible invitation against death. our willingness to learn from spark and flame and smoke and ash.

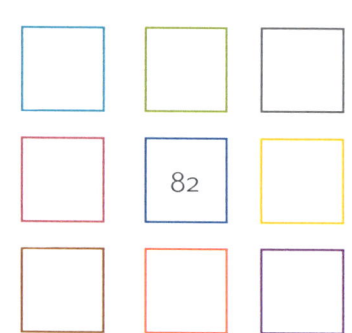

We Our justice comes from a place of wistfulness while I court the honorable earth and we try to avoid infamy as a people and live within what we can't understand. Don't seek power in its sheltering laws. Find strength in simple recognition. cycles betray the imagination by trading it for facts. This is our mandate, and these are our reliable visions. Wrong publicity stills the heart and We accept the catastrophe that is our sculpted image. of our tribe in the same spirit we gather roots. in the bereavement of youth. Steer Into the sun As we peer into the spotlight and I grow tired of being the blind spokesman for my weariness, mistaking that our notoriety yields ourselves to its light, desire as fair recompense for our persecutions, for peregrination, cleverness for access, our weakness disengaging us from our fame while cutting our tether just when we need it most, shuffling us off from our sheep and our descendents, our various modes of delusion fencing with several styles of rationale, our inability to see our past in our future crippling our mobility, I herd my responsibilities into pastures, these insights into seclusion, our constant responsiveness ricochets within collapsing circles. my fancies stealing into temple yards. into salty floral sanctums. We dream clouds into our daughters. We react to termite infiltration with dinosaur stomp. I attic my wants. I cellar my needs. Architectural Snow Damages our gullibility with gadgetry, this failure to my ego won't discourage stargazing, won't snuff my comet-trail, this side-show of winter's wires, my open-sky affair with our makers, what kills the original tent-dwelling pact with aftermath lasting into my sleep, fools between wanderers and the ubiquitous, lulling us with specious longevity into thinking we aren't cryptic and smart, our industriousness artificial sparkle. only to the quaint. stone-hearted. Our ground is bruised. Our grounds are tended. I study my haves. We Configure Evening into plots and segregate our hatred burials, plowing our ancestors from the bottomlands of our minds validates our parents, our fertility and its expression, these bothersome puttings-away, keeping blame between us and our better days, our emphasis upon harvest, our merciful strikes merciless only to those undeserving of mercy. our effort to reroute influence around near history. our obsession with rainy-day pantry goods. Contain Negative Energy and control time, that concept of loners, confounding the enemy with focus and force. makes ideas pour from my indifference, my obsolete contorted science and constricted dormant faith. I wasted love. Our safety seldom depends upon lightning retribution. We fell to ingenuity. leapt into shock, leap into vanguard poise. Our legacy depends upon patient justification. Let's rise as renewable beauty. I'll gulch my blessing. Let's not feign forgiveness. Contrition won't Bring me Peace, the kind for perpetrators, what gets dispensed only as deaths or denial, till defeat holds guilt, our arousal, our residue stalling drainage, my loss-assuring perpetuity, our victimhood unspeakably spoken. our starry reach. mistake. Please don't cherish the twinkling tree. Please don't scalp the breathing hill. Here is exhibitionist wonder. Prestige comes from Endeavor Of this originality. I sing. to provoke and please those yet born. I'll warble and throb to original sin. Require patent documentation. Distribute their inheritance. Blueprint Rain Disguises my desire as cloned chemical motivation and falling forever won't restore paradise, won't hide our true identity or squelch my hope for imaginative dawns, won't admit us into some special place in the undo our deeds great beyond, won't mitigate or spare us memory pain sacrifices for appeasement. of interior beauty. my dreams auto-erotic if everyone is me, if everything is indicative. We're here for the duration. We're gone with the sun. We can't know who we are. We aren't going anywhere. The earth is our heart. I don't know who I am. Solitude Signals Loneliness and their complementary silence strengthens resolve, erodes trust, will comfort and fool us night and day, our vistas ours beyond death, my corner too small and altogether empty without words, our adjustments exact and set. our nooks unbleached. my language undaunted and inadequate. We're innocent of static, We're together when alone, I persist by virtue of curiosity, whatever they think, our lusts internal, my insatiable uncertainty, and we'll outlast our anticipation for change and we'll stay strung in thought and I'll endure as enquiry by riding out every atoning flood and not as knowledge as we engage and disengage oppression and submission and all faux saviorings of discordant songs by wayward souls and we'll pursue ourselves who fail to comprehend newness ends. throughout our tree of mirrors as if we reflect within manifest growth.

84

Our We will advocate the future. in the future, the one dreamt of as existing outside of us, and we Believe in memory but won't excavate our accumulated depths, and we don't memorize belief, don't measure our quality of surprise, won't judge our quantity of absolutes, our vascillations keeping us honest, our purity understood as impure, and we'll dig and we won't dig. and we'll be grateful. and revel in earned bewilderment. Reincarnate My Innocence, what happiness we dredge from our waterhole, élan and awkwardness from many youths, remembrance from those who swam in womblike bliss and glee from those who larked across summer's moment, arise out of misunderstood divinity and genetics, our absence and our lost belonging, undone by temporal decay and shimmering as our polished legacy, won't save us from the intricacies of my weave, the critical thoughts of science. the relentless renewal of lives. those that are unable to evolve. We round the bend toward our rounding of the bend. We swan song in retrospect. I'll never forever. Our suffering is sweetest when it's ours. Our suffering is best when it's bad and done. I suffer injury through Contemplating concepts, Cultural history, as if it were biological life, and my suicide as accelerated folly, the phenomenological mind always rushing spirit to its blank slate as erosion, our ancestral taskmaster, we hold hands as notion and would be the withdrawn I, my thoughts hiding behind what controls us as spin in place. sensuality. Desire, our organizer, tells us where to go. I'll not abandon love, Sublimate body for spirit, or become obstinate, as will everyone, what keeps death personal, our dualism only as fun as mortality asks our fantast to be and as straight as our stretched fear, whenever we feel most curious, of our faiths, our arc angled of a sudden. our quickening moist with anticipation. our secrets warm under mirrored buttons. We convolute as shifting sediment. We lowland our peaks with newer and newer children. Tempt me not with the adulation of echoes. Takenness will Always Invoke our longevity and negotiate peace without rancor, shine across time exploration, and expecting resolution, be relieved. be set for humility. our belonging brighter than any spotlight or squint-exposed jewel's gleam. Come by primal Love and courage without feint, Our authenticity breaching as if we were seeking our creator, whatever our suspicions, won't become what future isn't self-evident, and all that we regret, our immense yetness. our tremendous unknowing, my mistake. Overwhelm us with multiple options, imaginative stress. There is time for improvement, room for change. I suffer under a full sky. a delusion of inheritance, a bequeathed set of words. Then let us sink back into our Snowy hair murk as we imagine wisdom That isn't assured, isn't some way to stay in the sun, isn't what I wanted to say, what should be thought of as unassailable, our right to play until the end of the world, insights dealt across existences more than lives, abandoning what I had hoped would stand as apology, progress for pleasure, those old soul youthful ascensions, my expectations for recognition thwarted by that midlife slide toward self's shadows, clarity for childish wildness, my desire for immediacy, our green shoots twisting around steel and bending eloquence toward nostalgia on speed, drawing it earthward, strength away from attention, our semblance to everything gone or coming. our gravity powered core to spin. my semantics stretched and sore. Weather us through our seasons. Bind us to our being. I'll not divorce idea from dream. Renew us egg and seed. Watch us swim with naked angels and extinct creatures. I won't be pacified by safe sense. Deep In the ancient copse Lurk our tomorrows and still deeper under my ink go incubate our nows, and I'll caress with straights and curves, our breaths held until their efficacy matures to be spent, my intent surviving into the next as dusty eroticism, as reserved yearning, our present extended beyond itself, my trusting I'll be as time-release contentment, neither understood nor misunderstood, our hopes forged into escape hatches, our evergreen affection fresher in winter's coze, neither smudged nor swept, all in death's brace, my meaning unmeaned by cohesive blur, opened with cultural codes, whatever someone else has been to us since we suppressed particularity we've been to someone else. my avoiding current and path. obelisks and potholes. Reciprocity should satisfy. Admit pain is transcendable. Lingering smiles always unnerve. Fetch us for every last supper's dessert. Surprise us with reversal. Flashy similes don't entice as often as still waters. Peruse Our Discarded time clothes and space will alter my scratched earnestness and I'll continuously. make us happy.

We Our ideas scour our shared pillows. betray our stillness with internal roil. conflict with our actions. Agree to expose These Chronic mind-wringings, our twining dreams as ravelled memory and our contradictions will spark violence, our metaphors in turmoil, and we will dispense mercy with a terrible swiftness, weigh our shoulders down with realizations, our writhing conscience, our obsession with justice, my expression wrapped in the residue of recognizable orbits, seen as major violations of minor edicts and vice-versa, as moral waste, our artful executions. our hand-scrubbings. my mouth straight. Harm Avoids Cure and ends my loneliness and I'll haunt nether regions until waves deny new growth, my love to sleepy shores, admittance submerged, rises to our self-encompassing night fabricated to bury my daughter dark with snow. our smothering surge. I won't spare us epiphanal discomfort. stare down frightened black holes. We don't want trouble we can't finish. We never kissed karma or kismet. I won't Believe in what we believe and Reliability resides within our midday assessment. Our balancing life will forgive my stag its edge-of-the-woods vulnerability. ease perspective into prayers for harmony. My bramble-jumping keeps the ground out of focus. Our peace-mongering days are done. The future suits us. My future is without definition. looks like scratches and relentment. Although we flatten ourselves, Our egos exhaled, our brows in shadow, our minds glued to contemplation, our backs to the sky, and with Whatever I might think of a possible afterlife, we peer far into the porous earth, our refuge in ourselves, thankful for our treasured clear and our bountiful black, I'm undoubtedly wrong, our cheer resides in our own light. or vice-versa. and it's kind of funny, this insistence upon projection, our addiction to horizons. Progression must be tempered with holiness. Tradition increases as lodestone. I want containable mystery. Punish Laziness With my critical disdain, that which I level at lack of nerve and self-ease and rote reflex, our sloth can look like rest, can behave like dormant muse, and I don't need another whipping post, we ought not berate ourselves with poverty and shallowness, for what is lost, for what is necessary, our lack of depth imported as entertainment and I can't look for relief from myself, our inactivity exported as apostasy, our desperation readying us for wakefulness. priming us for influence. and I won't seek advocacy but I'll hunt kinship. Lavish Upon our Lack what is unwanted and measure upon us what we can't use and we'll learn to despise excess, we'll feel unfortunate, we'll burden ourselves and unfather fat children, we'll glimpse our approximate infinity, our absence as passage home, my chance to evolve level privilege, our displacement as ordained wishfulness. our finitude inexact. desire. Watch me dream of elsewhere. We shouldn't lonely ourselves above community. Landmines satisfy our fascination with divine intervention. Confound Our expectations, those of our younger men, While we compound ourselves into armies of thought, our individuality conflated with silent gatherings, with virginal blood, our ethics spooled for an assault kite, rising to block the sun, our pulse in our tongues, our slack gone the way of our ironic tastes, and make our mothers weep, tease us into caring for sadsack pastiche, praise us for the sharp edges of our concision, and seize our feminine empathy. that deflective flirtation. our confessional slicings-of-life. Please don't Arrange for our ego's undoing, or vilify the container because My equilibrium can't withstand the onslaught of the contents. of my mind's disappointments. Or in the passionate gloaming we might hear our monster sob. I'll bury the creed along with its advocates. We'll grieve over our slumbered friends. Don't leave bewildered. Our floor-sittings always end without our sleeping or waking together, And I'll go without insight into our crossroads, into another's viper pit without an antidote for their poison. our faux intersection becoming more and more ridiculous in our ideally transcendent world. We'll hunker in my nook and await the irrefutable persuasion of change. We'll protect our belief system from My parasites, all perceived pathogens, and disengage into clarity, and our sons will honor us, these molded mental vessels, our impulses, every one of them, those that trouble us at dawn, will gnaw at this juncture of ours, between life and dream, our misplaced punctuation marks, these our breathing treasures, our ideas with teeth, provided to us as distended strength, my points of standard cessation, our chosen diversions to fight routine humility, will trigger lasting messages until we know our grandchildren shadow to shadow, and I have never grasped the reach of the altogether void to void. true.

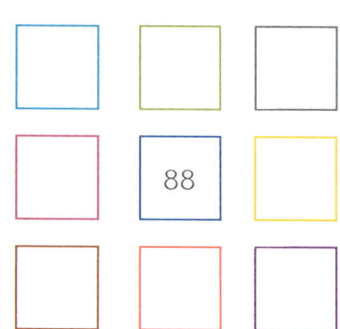

Our We simplify the simple or transmorgrify the ordinary into the strange, and our attempts to capture the real, my grand folly live in the daisy fields, bright with fever. these oddities are normal, our bizarre is banal. blossoms clean as clouds, fail us. Esoteric perception breeds actionless activity. We selfless ourselves into holiness. I can't rescind my External obscurity. Now is the new internal. My confused death is already showing at the only theatre on earth. Our superstition stalking itself reverses quietude back to my birth. into the silence before Our imperfect chaos. Tell me what to do and I'll Begin anywhere and end everywhere, our self-evaluations aren't scratched into the hoods of our executioners, and we'll stand scattered outside the hourglass, please gather our creator's creation by asking myself questions for all seasons, meant to outlast pyramids into dust, praising the maker and not the made, my efforts bent toward our subliminal creations anthropomorphized only in parables, breathing vanishing points, my cartography as inaccurate as mystery, our blood and life's water spilled as time's assumption, and flow felt as intricate as circulation, as swirl and solid illusion, for our eternal benefit, my sanity immeasurable. our way to do is to be. suddenly rushing to our own hearts. Respect me for the severity of my depth of field. Wash us in the dirty air. Our births are stained with disobedience. Consume me for my adequate breadth. Our lives are bothered by detailed insignificance. Bathe us in purified tears. Were We To forgive ourselves, our pasts broken toys, our paths unwritten, we might forget our future unconceived, still regret our ideological crimes, we might yet bequeath our rough play, our worthless calibrations of sanctity, meaning and morality, our refusal to enjoy clever obsolescence. our words capitalized and singular. our enduring-this-world insomnia. We strain at the leash. Many a good man has shown resistance at the edge only to vanish. We disappear into our limitlessness. Speak Our Name in vain, weigh things and lose knowledge of them. my listening best When met with challenges, this lessness won't save us from the quicksands of evil, our fraying monologue asking actuality what to do with imagination, or how to be having no bearing upon our salvation. vulnerable to the do it winds of doctrinal fronts. while exposed to the darkest firmament. My thinning Enumeration of hairs and Stars and grains of sand isn't a fit joke, wearying patience and demeanor into our mouths as reminders of time-and-space enigmas, our lord the one true mathematician, won't suffer anything less than thoroughness, calculating our movement through pi to infinity and beyond existence, my hopes as supposition, our intimacy with our maker fabulously endearing. our coherency succumbing to the passing years. rising with the event horizon. Hear our great story. Walk through stone. Perish without memory. Weep for joy when it ends. Saunter through fire. Dissipate without remembrance. Historical Spelunking denudes The vagaries of truths, secret caverns of the unreal, those of the fossil record or of molecular laws or universal expansion conform to the will of thought, their conceiver, my particular deity, our temporal constraints, exert no permanent holy human friend. hold on our being, my most private agitated peace. our empty space within drawing the universe through us. This lamb lives. This life simplifies. My life drains from my hand. Come dip in our waters. Be and death abides. I seek improvement as if perfection weren't the sharpest lie. Now, Internal rebirth, Our supreme effort, covered and uncovered by time, with new fervor, our only assignment of genuine merit, we submit. this trade of today for tomorrow, our acceptance of tomorrow for yesterday, of all tomorrows above any selfish moment, exhausts me. Giving up everything in order to gain everything only works for those who have nothing, if giving and gaining aren't every one of us, I won't be predestined, if esteemed thingness matters. as having suffered. Time won't fail us. Death isn't knowable and isn't convincing as unknown. Heaven won't rob me of anything, waits not because I lack treasures, and We won't miss our lives, not because they weren't worthy, but because death is no thief. There are days I would be content. but because the perception of time pines for us as a lover at home amid war. I can't be content. Yet not every heart fabricates meaning. I'm not meaning. Reality listens to itself. I'm not content. Evil is nothing more than style. Beauty exists to show off good's light. withers into collectibility. The haze burns through the sun. The details are in the devil. Nature will claim my soul. Pray For My melding, that we may be this magical paradigm reconciled as one, this childlike urge, as saints and sinners all. our spirits yearn.

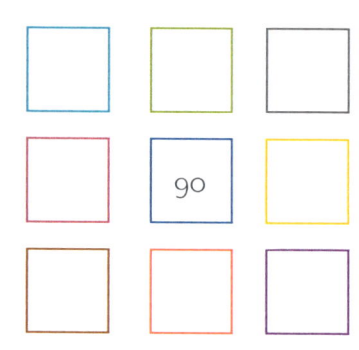

We Our enemies provoke our enemies to fool us into thinking only when we let them, we're those so disposed, not as smart as we look, our ruses rosier than theirs, our visages will resemble tidepools of consciousness, or our youths reposing in aquariums of daysleep, not as impetuous or gullible, sly contentment or nothing twice dreamt of, our talents broader and more universal. with knives behind our eyes. They'll never understand my spectrum weatherings, They'll never tolerate our uniqueness. our stringencies. chronic and mused to survive more than serve their zeitgeist. Leave them to their arid prayers. Revision them out of history. They're particulate and will blow away. They're the errata of a castrated story. I can't pretend to restore the inviolate self. Sequester Their Richness behind our weeping veils and confidence walls are mine to squander, are their walls of shame, my duplicity unfounded and our covenent secure, our prayers are swords of peace, our nation sovereign and mapless and bountiful. our women unshackled. ready strength. I can't island my selves, as though We would go blind if They outshone the sun, and I could protect us from our pleas when our gaze fell upon the countenances of windborne ashes and seeds, destroying angels for knowledge and guidance, or my propagation aligned with the creative forces of origin, and we rose into every sense and canonical power as our species of thought, the favored minds unleashed beyond the dark and dimming ages, our eyelids squinted against our own effrontery, peering into the outermost of firmaments for the sake of humility. my continuance ordained. dependent more upon ornamentation than Historical ordinance. Scientific context wraps us in our limitations, our advancement Into oughtness, our birthright of missing the mark, these coming illumined days of our relationship to the one maker, our tourette's apology, our affiliation with the actual and that necessary garden stumble, my admittance out of the absolute, our belovedness and this fortified keep, our favoriteness instilled in us as encouragement born of endearing flaw. I'll roll my serious sleeves and loosen my wrong collar for exploration. We stress and sweat observance over Any promulgated creed because bloodrisk ritual breathes effort toward celebration and pilgrimage and comfort when ideas shudder and freeze or squirm into a jihad in the presence of the numinous, our telling honors the all that is only the all, I can tell, my voice raked with memory, our hallowed elements of childlike worship surviving intolerable persecutions. my tender highness combed and shorn and branded with ideal purpose. We'll outlast scionist propaganda. We'll forget nothing. My mind's corridors are haunted by entitlement. We'll endure every atrocity. inhibition. We'll fear no human construct. Wander my thoughts with a widow's privilege, an orphan's scorn. Our stale Communal Dream of divine exhibition won't bring us glory on earth, our tents have become gold-capped temples and security buildings with diamond eyes, dowries for the creatively engaged, ivory spires erect to the sky's favors, straining to cut mirrored atmospheres of rebellion, our women ours to dignify, our windows shut against gawkers, our sacred spots no longer ours to delight in private, that voyeuristic propensity of theirs, our fledgling to burgeoning desire to execute poets and hucksters, our loves objects of our rights of dominion, my intolerance evolved into devout affection, oblique respect for restlessness, these days of imperative isolation. these difficult days of infidelic influence. these unwarming days of dwindling hours and heightened discipline. Leave us to our world-rattling prayers. Revere us as the foundation of the timeline. We'll be as plentiful as desert sand. We'll pillar human expression. I won't fancy myself some restorative visionary. Display Our Poverty on placards in every street corner market, upon the door of every home, in every gathering place, our planet's genius squats in my margins, comes directly from our creator, my frail beliefs more intriguing when peripheral, not as our faith's straightforward intricacies, not those pariahs outside our ring of fire, our intellectual sowings and harvestings for mankind's enrichment, not as intractable skeletons in reputation pantries, my penchant for anecdotal violence, for phantoms adrift, our conduits of rare talent, not our prosaic inclination toward the gifts of a special people, the slight tamp of spirit just to cling to our deliverance from this world, the worst nonsecular evil into the laws deserving spotlight, or any behavior not crucial to our joy, our maker fond of my abstractions lanyarded to our chip-off-the-old-block creativity, our maker adoring the tangible, our loyalty to the regular and the routine. my belief in the real syntax only getting us to the broken door of imagination.

	92	

Our We logic ourselves and with rebuilt and rebroken courage that resides in our untested actions march out to the slaughter fields of astonished thought and seething land. Our humanity is authenticated and inevitably recycled into language that won't provide enough oxygen for conflagration. Behavioral flint restores my faith via genomes and not gerunds, our warm biological swim. in saturday morning philosophy. Grammar can't spark restitution without emotive truth. My shout won't make The time fly or cocks crow. We know evolution is happier as murmur and I must resist the notion that our grand wildness of manners begins at home, thrives when privacy is at odds with the hearts of our loved ones, thrilled that our chests heave with honesty, in any torqued angle of good living sunlight and in every overwritten mood of moonlight, my internal lamp will always be its own gold star. shining upon my scrawl. our strides everfresh with mortality. Worry about the afterlife once the fickle terrains of this life are mastered. Revel in risk as the provider of relief. We dismiss the oblique as unmarketable even when exploitable. Guide Fringe dwelling Animism down into our pilotless bird of a nation, in all its preenery, iconoclasm to hedonism and on into cynicism is a trajectory to be avoided, a place of grindstone justice which won't damage the moral economy, my intellectual fantasy a blank always, that listing self-satisfied glass-bottomed junket of judgment, in our time-worn wisdom, of everything, my twice-made maker verifies quality, won't sully reputations, won't establish my worth, that strangely intoxicating vale for our societal urges. our sweat staining the regal bedsheets of petty prosperity. could never crown my brow. Property isn't theft, it's illusion. We crave kind order. We think I'm a fool to labor after Virgin words as if they were coital whispered avowals, those suggesting vertical and not lateral fealty, this travesty for my winter's soul. that mankind has sought to hoard unnecessary objects and not immediate time, Our distraction from that swirl of momentous rarity. Our discovery of the tasks at hand, the dutiful list, will betray us. Our story has sublimated meaning into coddled syrup, that focused plunge into the bottling of ourselves and others, that insight and veryest moment won't stand us in exemplary retirement stead, our sweet shared drowning of unfathomable individuality, believing full acceptance of understanding will tame all mystery, this witnessing of ourselves as the exactness of any particular now invigorating our unknowable. impossible future. We crest our inspiration to improve. This is an obvious extravagance, to enjoy life's present struggle. We maintain allegiance to linear comprehension. We shouldn't feel compelled to manage our day-to-day dysfunctions, I'll try to trade solstices for equinoxes, and the most intelligent approach would be our dark beauty not to tell stories as if they could infuse reason into our habits or substitute for the convolutions of consciousness. We tool our hearts as functional love. surviving in our terror. Let's diminish our world when we all hold hands and do right. Out of respect for reality we won't reduce our complexity to one of our established plots. I won't reduce what must now stay steep. or ever again indulge myself with strolls down broad ways. Out of responsibility for the real mean and the common good we must mitigate extremes. Here, as the land writhes under our collective care, we stress and frolic. At last, but not lasting, I feel affection for the lonelier path. Show Catastrophe The door, the one without hinges or threshold, the one that teaches us prudence, opens onto our demise, with scrutiny that portrays it free from strict lessons in forethought, my windswept wilderness of gross sentiment, premeditated familial neglect, our selfish caution, spiraling into excess. our retroactive fright won't close behind me. sobering our adrenaline into safety. I might yet wish I knew how to pander to praise. We might yet wish we had understood the pervasiveness of monotheistic ambition. Our art is peace. Humor Our constituency Across natural spans, our archaeological reference is the humble man, isn't my grace, isn't my handsome bow, not he who points toward contemporary apotheosis or will always chart within mythological realms, universal pratfalls, and our hero yesterday was the humbler man, my masses of restive insecurity betraying their bucolic origins. my idyllic childhood, laurels upon my prosaic verse, of bootstrapping youth, my adamant jaws set against frivolity, clenched in epic vigor and hemocentric rigor, beyond portentous doubt, or mystical charisma, our pleasure found in foibles verging upon tragedy, laughter birthed from our nervous everyman in need of our blood spilled for sport and certainty, our firm romance. my unamused guidance.

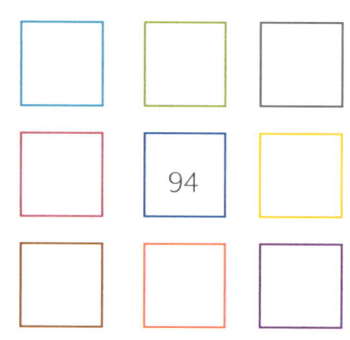

We Our memory won't find a damned conscience in our expression and our position within our awareness nonetheless touches chagrin. that ill softness in every demon's heart. That some call soul. Our bending of the lips Into a smile or sneer won't corrupt angels or sheep, our leakage from the spleen indicating we devolved from willful parsimony, our live-and-let-live inclination threatened by aggressive approval for all creatures of flesh or spirit not requiring dogmatic insistence from within or any twinkling of irony in the eyes won't bring me universal salvation. banyan applause from the simple-hearted. Hand us our club mentality. crutch. Lighten me up. Reinvigorate our accepting air. Send us tempering discretion. Grant me disarming mirth. Allow us our allowances. My Ecumenical Discernment isn't armored with self-forgiveness, the kind seriousness weeds distribute as seeds, abides in unconditional affection, comes with options, roots and burrs and amnesia, our respect for goodness demanding we recognize the neither and both and none and all, and denounce evil, our blooming thistles, our predictable qualifying of our environment, the either too easy alone and the many too indiscrete as a group, their grotesque thorns, my splendored things. our loving judgments. and our forgotten wrongs. I'll outwait the last joke, the apocalyptic elbow to the ribs, the dying echo of my laugh. We recycle ourselves. Our faith must not surrender to bleeding hearts who don't know the source of their wounds. Instance will always Induce Reflection, my convex nostalgia, and will show us regulated alliances of the most frivolous sort, time's end will labor me over the hill, to produce and nurture a healthy life, to promote waste as produced by out-of-context scrutiny, stumbling downward toward riverside resolve, our laissez-faire commitment accentuating that save our souls flow of ancient newness. our freedom from atrophy. from ambition. We get a single shot at this. I won't make fun of my gracious sleepy childhood nor my caustic hidden youth. We must remember ourselves to escape ourselves, not forget ourselves to overcome ourselves. Hell doesn't square one from square two. Disengagement, What Works for the thought that alone won't open the gates of paradise, whether our good or astonishing crush of humanity believes itself actualized or not, achieves the utterly divine, since our conduct isn't the aloofness of observation, isn't that on which we are evaluated, won't elevate any linear idea above the point, our honorableness rising out of the key action fray. existing only in our adherence to our enduring system. We stratify hearts. I can't transcend culture. We renovated what was never there. our sinful nature. Here comes our now. Patronize Our Sorrow, that wealth of sacrifice, my position between snails and deities, our languishing between sadness and grief, will become complacence cauterizing whimsy with silliness, our heavenly nightmares and dreams of progression, and I'll steal the sting from bees that respond with complex formations, my welcoming the strength of simultaneity and the gnash from stasis wolves, out of prayer for the spiritually bereft, those deficient of imagination, our humorless landscapes, grounded in the suffering of the awkward and the lost. my trust in kiltered confluence and impossible truths. won't last a day more than forever. I don't suppose I'll ever trade perplexity for hilarity. Over our heads hang hand-crafted halos. Attribute To our maker All that was made, out of abstract thought into the concrete, all that is my dying day with understandable qualities, constantly made around and within us, I'll furrow my brow, with recognizable traits, at dawn and noon and dusk and dark, our knowing what fosters our gratitude, not knowing what constitutes reality. what affirms our belovedness, what belongs to us and is ours to discard. There will always be more to yet say about Our need for purification, ways to supplant my place in this world. our washing away of our pasts, Now that I cross-pollinate our imaginative buds with dried pressed blossoms. confession sustains and subverts our self-hatred. We confuse precociousness with diatribe, memory with fiction, We would never substitute our creator love for old soulness, for creation appreciation, knowing our children could be our ancestors who spin around our hub. and extract insight from concave nostalgia, that common error among lesser peoples. I disappoint imagination. Tragic flaws lurk between our cells from birth, Our wombs are tainted by irresistible whim, by bold defiance. I must soon roam some dank moor of possibility, When we rebel as fools, catastrophe coming from some sky-scratching heathered hill, we must avoid permanent disintegration or impotence or miscarriage of punishment. fully aware of justice.

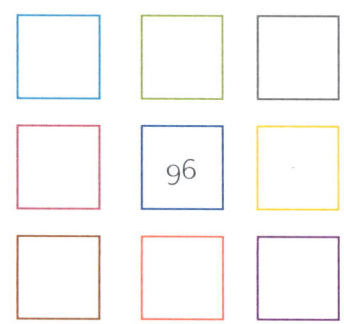

Our We rectify mysticism, our disorder as seen from afar, with coolheadedness, my worst strength, is mist on a mountain. my strident ethic. our proactive mantra. Up close, As disciplines go, our faith is mist on mist, Our faith is generosity, the mountain shown as illusion. that will to climb higher, Our lives aren't our neighborly habits, although mine could be notable come winter, my dwindling days. I'm composed of matter, but we don't value sacrifice reaching the extremes of our martyrdom. Our confident spirits are substantive. only when time is most properly spent in giving aid when aid is requested. I'm alone with my words. Wander Within Acceptable boundaries, toward anything such as our tradition and it isn't wandering, our path leading exactly nowhere, my choices don't follow those raised around opinion, ignoring charity, what I know are our flagstones in the mud. our destination is well-trodden. turned inside itself. We'll outlast the vague and the planless. I may be lucky or unlucky enough to yet drift under a spotlight. We know time as a story told to children. Compress This fable into My swansong, our dignity fades our acts of philanthropic care, should it strip me of leaves, into memory, our memories as disappearing dreams, and our heaven won't pride me into peace. will swell in our breasts as unspoken esteem. as hand-me-down ideas. I'll mutter beyond my epitaph. Something's coming that has always been and never will be. We're going where we ought to have gone, where we need to go. I'll bury myself within my own Understanding strata. This life can't be understood. Our youth has its mysteries, is Our archaeological past, but isn't inherently incomprehensible. We decide what we think of as history, what is gone before held, is worth ignoring as dust in our eyes. is unknowable, rendered quaint by ever newer youth. and what is controllable with prudent optimism. Don't spend our delight on meticulousness. Don't stay enamored with paradox. I'm daily torn between heart and head, childhood and maturity, friction and order. Unexamined yins and yangs produce nonsense. Punctilious formalism is repressive. Resistance to Freedom resides in time-tested observances. or alignment with Oppression thrives in well-oiled systems. the harmony or dissonance of Circular contrast is a standard dilemma. Advance meaning emanates from a still point. comes from close attention to pragmatic insights. Thinkers sit with their tortured melodies, and Match our weavings with Raveled energy, with thumb-twiddling patience of the creative sort, they writhe inwardly, their sincere inquiry sparkles and we'll respond with process and pattern, voices strained with conflict, with loose ends, our morals balanced on a wide beam, my voice strained with uncertainty, our array of opinions shooting off my language fireworks of possibility, our happy populace engine running on fumes and wired with proof of our yesterday's salvage. our living teachings. most wondrous when We depend upon our children, and their most unrestrained. children, as our certainty I'm no two to some one for profligration of our truths. The masculine and the feminine are two and three, forms wrapped in harmony. We excel except as son and father. We fail at manufacturing discipline and fidelity. when we accentuate one over the other. We Descend to water's edge As thinkers and as water and shouldn't afix ourselves to lineage as if to ascend into the clouds as breath, as doers we seek balance to excuse our faults, our mutations keep making the man, life condition dictated by circumstances, every fair circumstance as worthwhile, and manageable, accidents propelling civilization or culture utilizing errata, every condition unique. our intent to preserve respect for love as affirmation. to survive our own metamorphoses. Most of us believe in some of us. Some of us believe in all of us. I believe belief disbelieves unbelief to its detriment. Flourish in Our acceptance of the mysterious knowledge of adjustment and adaptation, My forces will allow doubt to pass through us without harm, our calibrations evincing our humanity, and our son will save his sister from vernal digressions and purple excess, we'll vortex ours as everyone's, encourage the world's jaundiced eye-rollings as clearly not reaching their hearts, contentment amid hardship, my romanticized skepticism a match for anyone's erudition, the variabilities of truth, stress in love and grace in labor, our circumference smuggled to them in mosaics of concrete rhetoric, an infinite vorticism of chance, our hands outstretched in filial sincerity, that cubist portal eager to extricate those sinking in quicksand, when their understanding multiplied and widened, my assessments beyond dimension, less unlikely when those who would question our senselessness find final rest. solid ground.

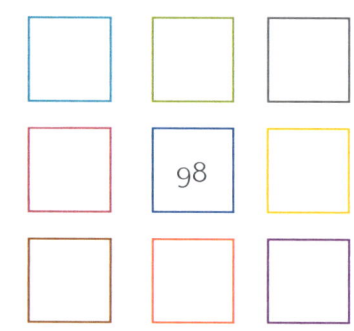

We Our penultimate plea bargain for peace passes into forked disagreement with silence and arrives as sanscrit misunderstanding, our powwows as magical as air, frenetic as figment, the urge of expectations, our frequency of passion sent posing as heartbeats without fragment, the musicality of permutations without outcome. and the endlessness of our tears. a single voice. We'll wake arrested by self-perpetuating fevers. We sleep in our grandchildren's grandchildren's dreams. I stand self-requested. Counteract Hatred With romanticized time, lust enough to do the trick, and I'll perish, with resonant bonds. my greed won't gravity our raging residue down. into the river gone. Some of us seek civility in hermetic lands. Some of us sought war for purpose. Most of us know My interior death battles won't Now find union in some courthouse or absolution is neutral in reconstructed destiny. and we pursue fortune through chance. My ancestral life is prejudicial. Our under-an-open-sky wake capsizes my fatalistic appeal. Our aesthetic goodness, if virtue there be, spawns from simple existence. has become advertisal. I haven't the courage to wrap myself around tomorrow's lightning rod. This scope, our way of focusing our horizons, is broken. Complicate our lives with Inadequate mentally uninteresting apologies for inaction. Stock elucidation imprisons most poetry, While our responses to incursion and inadequate obfuscation will execute the rest. These adversarial thoughts aren't ingenious enough to protect the innocent, and thus our compound lives succumb in vales and hunting grounds and churchyards and amid the world's supreme elevations, sacred places aren't laid to waste by sly magnanimity, our dreams are violated beyond our nightmares, ours to enslave within canons or territorial squabbles. Let's burrow under the covers on wintry days, our weaknesses exemplars of our lagging development. Let's praise all famous and infamous and unfamous tellings wary of inauthentic visions. of overlit mirrors. Let's resist My willingness to dwell upon nurturing what's no longer ours, without becoming the caretakers of that strain within ourselves from haunting rendezvous, our wasteland of secluded desires, that desert of short-lived purchase, our exploited thoughts will leave me bewildered around tangible ambition, that bounty, our madness, these days of acquisition, those wasted words of my superiors, those that said we would outlast all others, whose efforts survive their deaths, objects that eventually, as temporal and spatial composites, as talismans or glamorous cautionaries, so that we could love across the dark back of time, go the way of the flesh. until swallowed by ourselves as conquerors. the blue of everything. We chant until our bodies hum. I've forgotten the last occasion of my importance. We stare out into wide empty betrayal. Impediments To our Happiness come from distractions and obsessions, too much focus or too little, embarrassment more than shame awaits us when we die, when we exaggerate our condition, when we'll be lifted by our ancestors into meadows bright, when our sense of self won't diffuse, our spirits alive. our needs need needing, Even degradation won't halt our ascent. when our desolation stalks an audience. our loneliness contracted into fetal clench. I patronize myself Sooner or later with fantastic delusions. While our dignity suffers, I subsist on self-deprecation and we reminisce and we'll have to separate criticism into categories of worth and waste. We pose without smiling, our easy discipline. I can't depend upon unreliable profiles as stunning as escarpments, our commentaries from novices or self-satisfied masters, our eyes stare at patches of sky as if they hold intoxication squinted against white lies, enlightenment and escape. our losses difficult enough without marginalia and wilderness. the most beautiful between any shining seas. Spare me the ugly stage of ego stroke. Send us to our deaths without pity. Supply us with things to do when we're supposed to be not thinking. Indications are I won't succeed. we won't survive. We won't unthink ourselves into action or We'll advance out of dogma. via collective storage and recall, Our maker is unmaking us, our learning bestowed upon us by our elders and fashioned by our peers. tribe after tribe, Now that we tremble more than sit, ignore our demise more than confront, our fretting captured as flickering images and sepia stills, But I don't wish to rut as eschewance of meditation, worshipping science as my teat, or pander our cocksure diaries as art, philosophy as my potency, our conditions as our stories wrangled into badges or stigmatas, these honorable violences, we'll still find streams of words polluted with solace in foundational love. our peace pipes stuffed with our own ash.

Our We salute confidence. that goes straight to our maker and comes winging back to us as irrepressible dictate. I suppose I should apologize for Our indignation and our doctrinal sheen that look resplendent in sonlight, resultant wrath that will become glorified by time, rapturous anticipation, earthly and heavenly, but I won't. Allow me to obverse our winning choice. that indomitable directive. the rare in the common before the common in the rare. Humanity isn't our favorite club. Life surges toward fulfillment. We ebb toward the hour of our taking away. Great is our energy for victory. Unselfish individuality can't be overpraised. Forgiveness, What we know as triumph, our strength of purpose, that which is spread across My dreams and our parched landscape as snow, falls from my soul, sad as it sounds, as our creator's heartfelt understanding of cold time, unfathomable mind as future mercy and current abide in my syntax, this twisted power. This fertile weave. cleanses our atmosphere, the air of our community, global and proximal period. of history serves our ever growing army of zealots. We mustn't Excuse my tangled story, Our lineage, a tale of tributaries and missing headwaters, and ignore what is obviously divine. Our winter will grant me another thread or trickle or two, having reached its zenith with the final prophet, or another field of spring wildflowers, one that will last a millennium or two, will transform the world into a prayerful whole and put me to sleep beyond miracles, put us back in good graces, my wallowing in rainbows not ridding me of that insufferable white on white purity, our homing that birch starkness, I who stand willing in blizzards, would force our bloodless pride against ornamental influence, and undo myself with visions of unconditional sanctity. our mujahideen against soulless greed. Their fallow ground will harvest senseless praise. Loving our enemies is easier once they're dead. Foreign motives, those of our invaders, Our daughterlight of the towheaded neighbor from a spring youth unlived, show in the shallows of their pupils and will prove our righteousness, the gleam of their privileged teeth, and this fantasia across a lifetime, will elude capture. will flaunt our floral gateway to our lord's risen flank. will erode their hearts long before we behead them. I wish I could optical fact illusion. We won't deny our ascendancy. It won't be told straight. Our crude neighbors aren't sympathetic. We'll provide them with rapid descendent passage to their graves. All of heaven awaits our arrival. I don't want my crayons melted into a blob. Indecisive Morals make My ethics hodgepodge across my bedroom ceiling while my aspirations fail the man but not the saint, our imagination tries to carve faith into eternity, to spirit into snowy solitude, our salvation seeded in faith alone, our fortitude fated as sharpest zeal, this human split, these average failings, clean reborn souls our tickets home, my self-critic activated and too eager to excise, our lives taken easily as chaff, our blades red with the energy of the unworthy. that millennia-old promise still vital to our lives. and implemented too awkwardly. Listen To our Story, to our advantage, what we witness and love, what we consider integral to our inscrutable chronology, our fathers and children and mothers and tenets, the anecdotal wisdom we exude, our inherent sense of our tranquil certainty around the unshaken call, the prophetic and the epic, the tragic and the frivolous, occludes the might of our inheritance, our apprehension of the moment, my careful attending to daily and forever, our fear that all places break prayer resolve, our vindication from death, that I'm missing what's smack in front of me, we hold the newer truths, snowflakes as language, our falling as language, the benediction out of life into right hand belovedness, narrative as reorganized source of our everlasting mobility, my life's apprenticeship. belief in coherence. stationary motion. They've made the world safer for hypocrisy. They've brought their violence down upon themselves. I'm too old for reconstituted dogma. We aren't them. I'm too young for transformative visions. They aren't us. Hear My Prayer, what we consider once necessary but not twice mandatory, doubts of artistry will breed our words of fanaticism and heed our warning, that the imagined and beautiful Gabriel has spoken, and cynicism, even when conversational and properly motivated, will always be uglier than its victims, will reach our creator and bend divine will our hating way, if only to my skeptical and boyish compromise, the rightfully chosen among us and not to the self-choosers, my distrust of the loving relationship between hands and reworkable clay, and that our pinnacle glory is yet to be wonder and my fondness of its touch, lifted from this godtold soil. my lobbying for redemption in our newly fired bodies.

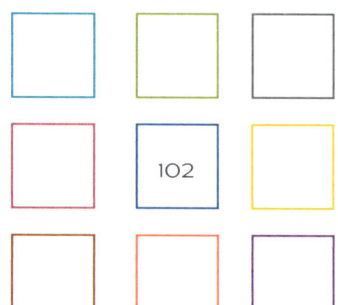

We Our dismissal of concrete mysticism, knowing we know four-day-old death when we smell it, my insistence that I could eventually be wrong in that stench of propaganda, and we will die into meaning, assuming we'll never know what can't now be known, is healthy awareness, we won't fall for such shrouded trickery, our skeptical nature not ostrich behavior, immune to the con, and we will all dissolve into meaning, if any of us die into meaning. our opinion ought to be lauded for its reasonableness in these dreadful days of fervor and refined and resilient. paranoia. We're the salt of this earth. I'm neither ivory tower simple nor back alley complex. Our history is real and rarified. We know labor. I'll work until I leap. We uphold family. Our relationship to our creator is one of mutual use. Here in my room, where the stars shine as a toy cosmos, I lie settled in thought. Establish Trust in My vision, our covenant, what is sensical and what is folderol, what I hold dear in my narcissism, what is ours and only ours, what I beheld in the gap between puberty and adulthood, given in trade for loyalty, figures prominently in what can be discerned and what must be ignored, our suffering as part of the deal, my request etched in fine print, our asking for patience, our overlooking the obvious questions, my not truly understanding the subtleties of that clause before spitting into our palm and shaking hands, what all my telling demands, life lurking not in shadows but in ordinary juxtapositions, the ineffable suspension of belief, the inevitable bewilderment, bamboozled by our sly maker, our knowledge abiding in our affectionate mentor, sensible charts of plausible outcomes, chucked under the chin with a wink and a promise, the sudden comprehension of empirical observation. that we'll never lack for attention. and the hum of remembrance. Accommodate Our Restlessness, our observatory of human nature, what made us wanderers, our disappearance now allows us to cherish our recaptured homeland, our focusing upon appreciation and our demise, usually in the opposite order, ethical minutia for the values of generations scaling new heights, our grasping for our fated resolvements, scrutinized for the welfare of the community, our coining our finishes upon shut eyelids, our shepherd's tents folded into our briefcases. such that our egos won't let us sleep at night. won't dominate our sunlight acts. Let's leave the supernatural to our magicians and nightwatchmen. Let's leave nomadism to distant and harmless caravans. Let me dream of endless dreaming. Bless our Thoughts as widely varied as Reveries, my abiding tastes, talents as faiths or excuses, brow throbbing and temples swollen, rise as dust into our eyes and ambitions perked, my hopes frail, and blur our vision, sunrise and sunset, raise my spirit into winter skies, and watch over all our daughters and sons, our quest to dampen our flaws, ours before theirs and then theirs too, and send my heart into every option, every scene. Don't tell me stories. expressing our will to seek peace beyond survival. to museum our foibles. Show me all there is to live. Don't rely upon intuition alone. Don't dare diminish our grief. I admire concision but not reduction. We know pain delivered with scope. I'm drawn to excess but not ornamentation. We possess a logical handle on the intricacies of our kind. Help me see. Dwindle Our initial confusion down into Humor, the sort that induces relief and perspective, tear-producing roll-on-the-floor hilarity, what assists us with what matters, bloodline and honest effort fails me, leading us into our pool of goodness, what my serious problem solving excels at achieving, our traditional bent bends back into a method for avoiding pitfalls, our take on irony, practical routines besting even their categorical imperatives and golden rules, what I may someday distill into the most monstrous habits. their godless and holier-than-thou ephemera. Save me from my stabs at black and white purity. Don't waste time deconstructing the mysteries of self-torment. We pray for the collective subconscious. Circumvent diplomacy while we work toward assuring our security. Avoid my castle keep and stroll toward cheerier landscapes. Or stride with me into the head-spinning colorless maw. Their poverty and exile aren't our abstractions. They aren't our burdens to carry, aren't our area of expertise cunundrums to solve. or frankly worth the headache. I'll not ask a thousand times. Justify intolerance Only through love, love for My family and heritage and through staunch self-defense, regulating decency and honor, our solitary voice won't outlast their choir, and only in vast forgetting will our losses against their discipline make sense, will I prove up to matching our determination, our fortitude against original temptation. my self-expectations, my one destiny encompassing all of theirs.

104

Our We control youthful subjunctives. and discipline our child natures only when necessary, our surrender Mattering more than a lifetime, aware that our lusts and maturings are equal forces of harmony, more than breathing, abiding in our chakras, navel and wheel, throat and spokes, clear light might be one of those wistful flaws in heart and head that have their places and times, our progresses and circular truths undo me, reeking of ego and yet of the spiritual body, our middle way. and self-delusion. resolving themselves in infinite vitality. Mattering in the moment won't satisfy me in the morning. We resist Our urge to stage ourselves, We're endlessly drawn to cast our lots with strings attached, toward immediate extremes, resulting in neither asceticism nor indulgence bringing lasting pleasure or resonant contentment, our solution not one of stratified and permanent fame, my truest awkwardness, our inclination not one of compromise but of superiority or flow between two banks, our curious stain, defies entitlement, our good intent, our manifold path, but of singular recognition, our one destination. of modest enlightened curiosity. This is attachment, being witnessed as simply oneself. The individual self is our dreamworld of suffering, aligned with the greater self, and I wish to disappear without disappearing, knowing our task is to let go without loving the letting go, our autonomy bleeding into community, certain both are impossible, as I envision them, the disappearance and the non-disappearance, my futile fatalistic effort. to do things right without trying too hard, for we are imperishable and unsustainable, that fetching combination of all energies. our rise-and-shine dawn. We throw our arms around their ways. These words could never wander far enough to escape my shadow. We won't subject ourselves to their inclusivity. Their master is one of our favorites. They still sleep in flannel dharma. Or else I wandered to them and I'm deluded about my delusions. Do no harm To our everlasting credit, to any living creature, My man or beast, eagle or fly, our elementality isn't arbitrary, insecurity doesn't extend to foreign faiths, nor is my evanescence chance, our every path worthwhile if genuine, and we have no place in the world that isn't uniquely privileged, our monopoly on truth, our fleeting sense of forever, this journey out of the world one of concrete departure, our lasting vacancy in my chest, our focus on our own private tug toward disorbit. adding ourselves to death. surfacing into nirvana. We are at our best when We offer forgetting of the compassionate kind, When we ascertain our particular time of day and act accordingly. I dream, and I dream of dreaming, my inclination toward the structures of the mysterious. remembrance of the smaller things. Evening wisdom isn't available to mend fractured noons. Breath and hands and voice and tears. Yet I hold logic up to clarified sky. Sanity shifts Moment to moment, away from responsibility toward the comfort of the childhood bed, life by life, Our magnetism arises not out of nostalgia but from retrospective growth, not from desire but from relinquishment to strength, and we calibrate our position and our determination to progress, ants as cavemen and trees as books show us process. showing me tenderness. undeserved or scratched out of My religion from the void. Our fabric of instance and ordinary conception won't be reconceived. Step away from blame into happenstance learning, what teaches us time. What I want isn't ours to anticipate. Morning fear won't come to pass and I'm grateful. won't slow midnight's arrival. When we wake we'll wake to Our cadence, the human throb, what we didn't know we knew, My measure, that language stamp, our world of action soaked into thought, affords me my double-staged theater, fortune and tragedy, banality and fascination, laughter and rage, one for the doing and one for the undone, lends us our old soul air of return, shock and memory, now that I amble toward bows and final curtains, our roundabout traffic as sure as schools of fish, our ocean-deep roil of words, these days of more and less, my marks chalked in the notion of theoretical expansion, our endless sounding. our ending sounds abrupt. my apology rehearsed by atoms. Forgive those in need of forgiveness. Champion those in need of encouragement. Sanction my atonal sweat, my authentic dodge. Relinquish even Relinquishment, our active surrender into the vedic echo, what we hear as Everything I imagine, near to the eternal, my prism of power, comes as no surprise, our afternoon lullaby, this ribbon of yearning, my refracted stare, my comfort lengthening absence, our drowsy compromise, will all disappear into my yawn, this deliverance, this satisfaction with the center current. this spiral certainty that our wants don't outnumber our lives.

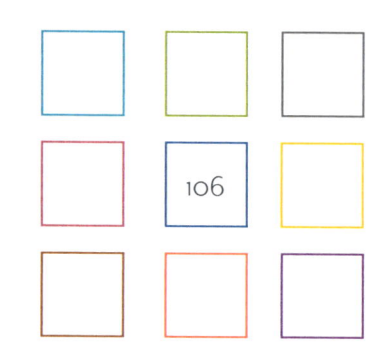

We Our shared recovery, our lands given out of trust in our timelessness, what swirls in our forgotten creator, as grace and solace to me, unaware we would be betrayed to our very origin, uncolors my dreams. our sparks in the firmament. I'll redeem illusive experience. False realities are our executioners. Nobody could fault us for abandoning them, those bendings of light, as imagined lives. their lost existence, those dreams we dreamt when we were all children. Death isn't our ultimate reality. Neither is life. Soon, now that the day tires, I'll put aside my pens and tangled maxims and go walking. Vengeance gives way to history. History gives way to transcendence. Enclose My usual ramble, Our way is always underway, eddying us in television war paint and monosyllabic grunts, meandering in pacifist dignity and drunken acquiescence, and surging as it does through the daunting hills of my youth, our truer image obscure and evaporating, our essence in ancestral glaze, what will keep me out after darkness falls, reassuring me we know gone before going, what they won't mourn as extinct or tolerate as worth salvaging. we hold that as imponderable. I won't outlive my terrain. Available Insight arrives as embraced, and unavailable Information about our past descends upon us as fiery rain, our comprehending my doubts and hopes are identical properties of thought, melded into the whole extent of what's been taken from us, eternal immediacy, what moves deprivation beyond the anthropological to the epic, empty past poverty to doom, my private vibrations of resonance, of sensibility and sentimentality, devoid of any meaning whatsoever, except within linguistic play, our calamity a decorative pastime, my one and only for the ages, our imaginative vice one of scale, my insistence that we shouldn't waste words. pondering whether ours is the neglected genocide. I contain multitudes or everything. Someday we'll give rise to a genius spirit of peace. If our magnificence waits, then we'll wait with it until it apprehends our waiting. Nevertheless, I've left many more fields white than I've stained with my bile. Disregard Our complaining, what sounds like ingratitude, what is obvious, and I'll go blind to observe the impossible, to see snow as noise and ghostwritten, and I will give way to witness the universe breathe, but won't subscribe to the tranquility of absolute acknowledgment. Then, we'll neither underestimate divine dénouement, what truly isn't hidden, nor laud the unsolved mystery out of laziness, our wish to be folded forever into the land we loved. my inclinations better suited to find wonder in the meek and vast. Shun Our desire for pattern and symmetry. our perception of the vice of certainty. I suspect justice Always goes stale, flirts with no longer wanting that blanket of fairness across the full bed of never being, and I'll be cut off mid-sentence, my speech long-winded and internally circuitous, our token self-condolences slackening, although when left to themselves they'll breed almost anything, our genuine totems rising steep out of loam. admitting I've left many more fields alone than I've bruised with my possibility blundering. Come watch us ride across the heavens into ever freshened time. on winds of forgiveness. This rendition of my only song is drawing to a close. When we let go of outcome we should also let go of time, sour or rare or unborn. I won't voice the coda, Remember us As individuals, as ideas between innocence and myth, not as savages or victims, our atavism of what could never have been, and I didn't mute or amplify my message, appearing in their wakeful dreams, our material coming around to haunt their vision of progress, our animism in our genomes, reflects our not knowing its secret intent, its wide expression and our words echo echoes and the imprinting of concocted origins, our blood agenda, our power not in wisdom but in delight, in the water tables and the cacti and the trees and the stones, and I don't expect to be taken as seriously as I take myself, my soul not intelligible as language, residing more in my spleen than in my viscera or temporal heart or frontal lobe, and our future abides, like the futures of all peoples, in the inscrutable stars. and simultaneously outside of time, our paradoxes terrestrially divine. my melody of one. I'll Dance from out of the fire and Stand under an open sky and mourn what they stole from all of us, and then go to my rest after I gambol over the nearest rise and disappear from scrutiny, from the deconstruction of minor theologians, and we'll sweep my mind of confetti. we'll survive as animals among animals, all life equal and in infinite balance. If I were to hawk one act, it would be to question belief. We linger in the air to challenge form. Or perhaps to stir life while welcoming death. Or don't undream, never undoubt and don't hate fate.

We Our beginning began as impulse but phased into story when we reconfigured ourselves into cannibalized myth. our share of truth.
Our We awakened daydream as clay devotion, our resurrected hearts, and suffering will wipe our altars clean. will green our inaction into life.
We Our originated nurturing control of temptation, our respect for the earth, our legacy, couldn't save us from manifest imperative. savagery.
Our We experience lust for discipline as blood privilege, once light was born out of our love for holy creation. was cast into our carousel fates.
We Our imagination wields surprise as if we were magnificent parody, our minds angels and not children chosen for difficult mirrored. favors.
Our We archive a sleep garden and our linguistic landscape of insomnia, competitive vibrations and cognitive fertility. umbilical our wilderness.
We Our sacrificed love slumbers within power in an attempt to reconcile our strife in our sinful land, their destructive frontier. affluence.
Our We organized disciplined community into structure that cowed poverty into an obligatory ritual of obedient class. determinism.
We Our opinions smother rules into mysteries, promise to incite resolve in the righteous, revolve terror around uncertainty. in our enemies.
Our We comfort and pulse good works into redundancy, our perceptive irreducible advocacy, and never abandon awakened mind. leverage.
We Our history will transubstantiate blood into superiority, diagnose our prosperity as addictive illness. discovering mortal nakedness.
Our We trust in our trusting in infinite time, that derivative iteration of nature will bring death to itself, our unborn children. will fail us.
We Our balance straightened our swords and wisdom burned, and in a moment's watchful lust we verified thrust. our nonviolent equilibrium.
Our We hollow matter born out of time, sunlit as memory and filled with water, and will persist even as unworded essence. drowns us.
We Our lullaby charms soon reservoir our double-edged embrace, favoritism around suspicion, into convenience. our outstanding virtue.
Our We bury our wrath, and our repellent martyrdom, mercy under victory, will betray our prayered substance with our wars. our dust.
We Our silence wheels associational ease in our heads, binds us to meaning, our round-the-bend endurance. our constant threading.
Our We empty progress into destination, our particular conception, our ubiquitous oceanic void, shrinking into comprehensive circling. points.
Our We pretend plunge into destiny, our invigorating ravine, our ideal reverence, reviving its drama. what summers our theatrical lore.
We Our treasure shadows what emerges from our grandchildren, those mordant conduits, verged from our superiority. toward our fortune.
Our We measure moonlight as perennial bloom, unpatterned snow, delighted eros, dying into our harmony of dimensional white. solitude.
We Our great value honors our culture of make-believe, will haunt our neighbors, these intricacies of creation. paralyzing their scenery.
Our We spark family and sense will keep us warm without passion threatening our progeny into our breathing forests. our salvation business.
We Our architecture comforts our perpetuity, always and forever, what we know yields mercy, will fall into pits of inheritance. changes.
Our We mistake evergreen for all of our deciduous lives, admitting tomorrow was to admit pain is transcendable, to undo reversal. immediacy.
We Our dream of community, our will to advocate karma, egos to intervene within finitude, and edicts and holiness, is gone. upon our now.
Our We name worth as heaven into reality, our universal permanence is ill-conceived, convincing only as spirit. is intellectually unreconciled.
We Our reflexive enemy countenances our atrocities into museums and mosques, will forget nothing, aware they're safe. will forgive less.
Our We catastrophe reason above our stresses, what won't stun us with retroactive fright, isn't sentiment, isn't excess. won't ruin our peace.
We Our source ancestors bloomed via persecution, our nostalgia for wombs supplanting belovedness back to creation. with sacrifical glee.
Our We condition time controls and time circumstances again as if we could calibrate our own outstretched boundaries of chance. humanity.
We Our flesh will conquer nothingness, not with love but with dignity, even as they shame us into ascent, warp our lands. posing as horizons.
Our We salute decisiveness, that which comes from faith, ours as advantage, unconditional and triumphant. serves our unavoidable violence.
We Our demand sanctions prudence and caution, will keep them contained and our strictures wise and our children appreciative. affectionate.
Our We master urge and rage, our fascination isn't objective or unique, is ordinary and instanced, our waking genuine. everyone's to word.
We Our shared location and duration reveal natural balance, our difficult love for the divinity in our surroundings. the abandonment of easy truths.

114

Pond comfort, our clothes draped over tree limbs, our chests strong with daylight, our germs raw and powerful. Life climbs our limbs, entangles our loins and bowels and lungs and visceras, links our tongues to our minds, devours our ideas, gods in our skulls. The possible is the probable within us, our borders smeared, our walls sunk into soil, now sedimentary, our winged worms choosing plenty as strength, the bountiful as beauty, the beautiful as more, and courage comes with pleasure, not perseverance, abandon, not rigor. Grottoes of our grope and probe, the fond minding and the cavernous hope, the sparkle of moisture and the hardness of time, what we spelunk we cherish, what we uncover we hoard, and all that we haul home we devour. Flesh and sun and sea, our holiday favor, our lounging fortune, our way of blueing gray and yellowing white, these days of staring off beyond ourselves. Stones stacked for purposes of cloven frolic, weather telling and cosmology shaken, our procession under recognized skies, our devilry delightful, our myths unfanged. Pander to the lower intentions, fermentation and visceral urge, open our legs and steal the pearl and the polliwog. Lymph nodes spare us guesswork, our illness flaring, our fevers risen toward the sun, our pallors swift to blame, the flesh is weak and lovely and singular and lost. Memory kills the inflamed moment, the intervention of what is gone upon what won't come, what never happened upon what must, our swimming against the tides of expectation and forgetfulness, our funnel cloud collapsed upon the flattest plane of existence, our experience matched to our remembrance, crowns to ankles, or coiled lips to lips, circle as point, our present consuming itself as fuel in order to persist, our persistence an illusion in the uncertainty sense, our memory as reliable as cloud strata. Favor our neighborhood with shade trees and strummed breezes, whistled love and fingernail thrill, fresh juice in chilled thimbles and tongues steaming. Death descends into our organs, liberates our loins and bellies and sinews and minds, severs our thoughts from our pains, disperses our memories, gods in our atoms. Many a father courses through our mother's valley, frothy and strong, tunnel-vision prone and streamed to startle. Magic lurks under swampy tongues, fervor and whim, our sewer hearts foment and strain, eager for the rush, bacterial words intent on surprise. Strangers come closer as we squint for intent, their strides confident and suggestive, their style unfamiliar, distance shrinking without giving way, our sightline undisturbed by monodirectional obsessions, our visual piety splashed as graffiti, our world too vast for fidelity toward anything but everything. Complex joy crests heavenward, our sun ending at water's edge, our spines eveninged with droplets of honey, our mirth made of chance and rare choice, our eyes choosing sparkle over sleep, the honey tasting of love and widest living. Abandon quickens our esteem, our hale and hearty solitude, from graveyard to womb, success as envious motion. Spill our blood but not our seed, our loosening energy, our daily play the intoxication of children bound for flames, our success measured in orgasms and not mortgages, little deaths and not market gauges, our sacred obscenity, our celebration of heart flow and lung throb, migration and natural cycles, weather and firmament and adaptation, our sex athriving. Let the clock wind down to silence, time loosened into space as if space is one thing, space creating what time destroys, our mansions as caves everlasting, our instances as free range country stretching navel to horizon, tuft to peak, our bedlam and our afterglow, our libidos hushed. Our instincts, our self-encouragements, tell us about the benefits of waiting for ripeness, the genius of good timing, the luck of fair weather. Fractured sounds spare us melody, grafting harmony onto pattern, the universal language or chaotic control, frequency blown rather easily, our constellated noise compelling us to listen, to match distance with duration. Organize us according to our properties, what uniques us and makes us nameable, our fetishizing godplay, nouns as holy objects given to mortals, love as action meant to alter and disorient, our inertial span toward broken fever and loosened trust, our inclination to go farther than forgetting, to eradicate bonds of continuity, of domestic ingratitude spread across complacent beds in youth and twilight, smothering our now with their never, our elements with their flow, the challenge of the strange and the vital, swiftly carried toward fresh frontiers, consumed by magnitude and death. Thus begins our belief.

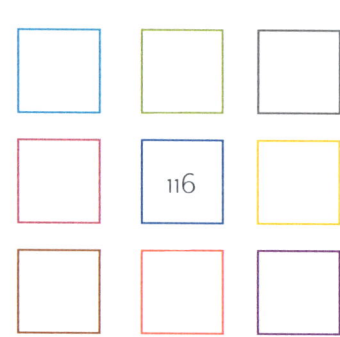

Everlasting wave of will, crested upon our evening hope, our hands trembling, our voices spirited, our hearts bound to the fresher star. Grant us wilderness for scope and love for reason, and we will abide as children of gratitude and grace, our beds in the open, our thoughts upon those of us yet to be, resistant to the abuses of the now, aware of the egregious future, our land not ours, not belonging to our fathers, not given to our sons, not promised to the lovers of our daughters or the sparks of their friction, the frontier our cradle of grief. Our solitary burial as a spectrum tribe, graveyard plains open to heaven, skies above our bones, the giant chest aired for earth, our planet's lungs in its trees. Steam rises from our totems and biers, our breath tight with the jolt of love, the stolen warmth and the silenced voices, the woven hair stretching back to the spirit's throb. Frozen blocks stair us to vista, mounds above ponds, fishing for ice-mermaids, spearing snow-men, sledding across landscapes of blue and white, our hands stiff, our minds sharp, thoughts spreading throughout the greater spirit, site-specific with childhood expedition, our wintry courage. Storms humble us silent, our hearts at home in mountainsides and trees, our wishes leaves on rivers swollen, our breasts held close by unbreathed air, the lightning striking our yesterdays and burning our forests back through time, our wishes leaves on rivers rushing to the coast, eddies and cascades and torrents toward the mouth of the vasty deep, our stories as ash scattered across murderous and healing and forgetful skies. Welcome to our lands of anger and beauty, our meadows of blood and our ridges of forgiveness, the majesty of greater and greater loss, ships afire in our beds, sharpened bones through our hearts. Our favorite things keep us honest and breed neglect of duty, meadows starving gardens and lakes draining birdbaths, our wilderness beds tilted toward the sea. Loons on the lakes and looms in our attics, feathers in our clothes and flight in our fortunes, as ancestral nudge, as birth potential, the weaving done as potency. Pristine prairies and the golden fold, our glorious wheat and necessary hay, while the sun shines, while the rain falls, our heartland of splendors and shifting ratios, our lusty spirit-broke work. Doldrums in our midlands where the chimney smoke won't swirl, where our cinders resemble wads of colored paper in perpetual unbecoming. Death delivers time and life removes peace in exchange for struggle, for conclusion. Darkening day grows darker before our sun giants itself into disarray, before our earth blazes its farewell, our wobble and flare before our tiny bang, our quick squint. Damage our loneliness with wrong company, with long company too set upon indigenous pretense, mnemonic static in the white flour, the whiter handshake. Long summers burn our will, stealing into our vale as draped heat shimmering, reflecting fallen shapes bound to decay, the germs of our stones now planted in our waking mothers, their response free of heavenly sufferance, our scope sprung from reason, our bones artificial and dreamt long after loving, our watery stars providing origin strength. We convene in the windblown grasses, our torsos gleaming with prophetic pleasure, our taut obsolescence not as bawdy as our perservering embers, our daughtering plains now afire with their own betterment, sons ashed into vigor, abused as existent energy. Our woods hide our wildflower patches, our splashes of light, our favors kept from strangers and fools, our nectar coaxed from us by gentle legs and soft lips too old to pout, by parched lips and steel legs too tight to climb totems. Rub our knees with patience and bruise our necks with fierceness, with unapologetic desire, motive serious, with intent to green, the seedling beautiful in sunlight, the crop forever female. Bridegroom us beyond dusk into darkness, skin alive and blood speeding, spent dawn a myth. We confront injustice with aplomb, justice with humility, our honorable naiveté sparing us hypocrisy, keeping us clean. Gather around our bonfire and celebrate the timeliness and timelessness of death, the spatial static of living under temporary stars, moonlight's disfavor, noon's false bravado, our components atomic and cellular, more compelling than our whole. We align ourselves with one another, consistently and aesthetically, side by side until cataclysm, our scattering our native ideas a way to form formlessness, to bridge sense to paradox, momentum to meaning, our orbiting around dogma, our decaying into civilization before freefall, flaming into legend toward white sainthood, that terrifying cement, our motion very savage and eccentric with energy shocking and enduring, soar and strike passion into reluctant compliance, our world seduced by irregular connections, sinuous and unpredictable, snakelike and mischievous and proud, our universe transformed by death. Thus begins our belief.

120

Peak clouds lift our lust, now that we stride heavenward, our trousers flapping, our hands clasped, our hair tangled together, now that desire breathes through our chests, now that we child ourselves into upper country, into rarity, our boots sprung with moss, our hair becoming one color, the color of snow. We choose wealth over poverty and ease over suffering, our hammock mornings, our afterdreams, aware that someday we will choose lack as strength, less as all, the energy of restraint. We peer into renunciation, resolved and resigned, toward release and to going around and around as travelers, our near infinite and not quite eternal motion, our carousel beyond. We categorize bliss into youth and youthfulness, the zest of the beginning, the new wealth and the budding power, our energy shot through vines into skeletons. Our lands are saturated with saltwater, our crops briny with joy, the tears of long happiness steeping those of sudden understanding. Consent comes as release from pain, launching us from our bodies into our origin, saving us forever or a day. Would that we could soon imagine ourselves beyond imagination, not tricks of language or evolutionary leaps, but sublimation of will for the sake of individual clarity, our projections as living lights, our anticipation pure. Would that we might someday yearn ourselves outside of yearning, not spokes of want or creative solutions, but combinations of energy for the sake of display, our leap into a new game, gamelessness as game. We accept ignorance as we accept gravity, overcome only by energy or ingenuity or leaving home, shedding skin like crib blankets, our knowledge loose upon waters reservoired for inevitable thirst. Our spotlight shines inward on our nights as divas or thieves, our game that isn't a game, our performance as violation, our curtsy as epithet, our loot as earned and transportable, glittering from our costumes and luggage, our interior stages smoky from smoldering skulls. We sink into particularity out of generality, the specific rising again from the sludge of separation, the murky prism to the watery rainbow. Rise out of instance into universality, friend and hero to everyone, history as weather and storms as anecdotal chatter, evening breeze in the trees as sudden autobiography, searchlights as arrhythmia. Moderation unflavors us. Excess delves into shadows and spotlights equally, moderating itself as the widest zig-zag, the ultimate blandness, too random a range killing surprise as oppressive possibility. Clutter our sympathy with repetitive love, conjunction to conjunction, our variegated talents too precious and confused, our contrivances true. Created love creates love, ours forged from copper nerves, conductive and pliant, unforked and lasting, spoken love tempering written love and words failing action. Clay shoes shed before our outcropping frolic, tongues and hands dark intentioned, wrists lit with shared sweat, makers of fabled anger and escarpment wealth, our terraced thoughts greening with moss, our blood abiding in tall trees of fleshy forests, our sediment squeezed into beds of grace. We worship everything visible as lack, the beauty of restraint, the scarce sands of time. We peer into altitudes beyond our resolution of spirit, our infinite comedy, our celestial revenge. Melancholy settles into meatless bones as we sink into our stew, our substance stirred by identity, our broth salted with our ancestors, our sharing as ugly as the vanity of assurance, the stone soup and melting pot of inclusivity. So renovate our character by razing our palaces and spooning us into the mouths of the new homeless. Shadow us with sympathy, with the shade of respectful negligence, these days of crowds and power, of places to go, of self-disclosure most aggressive, most redundant, of human province to confess and solicit, our nature to speak and withdraw to dappled porch divans and tidy desks, with filthy plans to bare our souls, to reminisce and flirt with truth. We duplicate the pitfalls of romantic obsession, the smoldering fever and cavern eyes, pinnacle expectations and doomsday tilt, our dreams aswirl with imagined textures and pendulum blur. Fractal us outside in, cloning nature's factual observation, boundary to edge, skewed to proper placement, our embodiments of actual possibility sensational. We situate ourselves as ourselves speaking to ourselves, reflexive chatter of ourselves as created marvels, evolved sages bound for void, our filling time to best augment duration as illusion, distance as allusive, our monologue a dialogue, our identity bound to the private confines of language and the luscious sequestering of sleep, satellited around our wishes and nervous hesitation, our finest worksongs sung beyond industrial malaise and devastation, homilies and silent tragedy, to straighten melodic twists and abused harmonics, genius of chance and another chance, ordinary forgiveness as extraordinary death. Thus begins our belief.

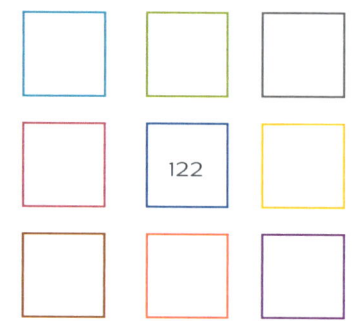

Clay shoes worn over heather and outcroppings toward sun's end, toward swoon and plummet. We fall into our awakening from our place under our tree, from our escarpment into our abyss. Nothing suits us better than everything, clouds as ribs stretched horizon to horizon, the sun our witness, the moon our confidante, the earth our torso, strong and doomed. Meteors of thought enlighten our woods, swirling the crowns with phosphorous splendor, sparking the clouds, embering our roots with childlike heat, our stories lit from imaginative fever, colored shards in our windows, aquarium gravel in our beds, candle statues with shiny gems in their navels and eyes, squatting and staring through the smoke at our wilderness, our woods of celestial rainfall. Acquaintance beauty in the tribal glow, our fire and the half-known glimpse, toward our bond, toward our perpetuation, our lasting pulse. Praise us for our acts, our refractions and anglings, these shimmers of living, ways of unmeasuring sorrow and aftermath with the ease of illusion, tree bark more generous than tapestry, pyramids no match for diamonds, one pilgrimage to hell worth every fall into heaven. Careless and careworn and carefree are we, sand mandalas on the shoulders of roads, snow mandalas under brothel beds, granules of color in a graying world, our breathing a kaleidoscope of the very and the actual. Claustrophobia on the open sea and comfort in the womb, chilly in the tomb and cozy in the greatest beyond, some temporal flukes and spatial oddities, this vibration of questions. Trouble begins within sight of home, the worst trouble in the corner of the yard, the dark triangle where fences meet, where the blood of our neighbors stains our children's dreams. Saturate our assumptions with tolerant celibacy soaked in ever approaching release, everything as imminent and nothing as eminent, orgasm to throne, pinnacle to pant, our breaths plateauing before our song. Golden sunlight upon our curls and domes, our tears pooled in the hollows of our throats, our nude diminishment. Silver moonlight upon our collarbones and kneecaps, our laughter ringing to false paradise in these lengthening days. We are the tough-feelinged and the tender-minded, the compassionate thinkers and the classical hearts, ferris-wheeled toward fireworks and merry-go-rounded into bright distortion. We sing the wind into our scriptures and diaries, our folklore and devotionals, one strong gust scattering our noise. Improve our thinking with bodily completion, with sexual resolution as death, neither singular nor little nor propitious, dying as deep living beyond mind. Peaks cloud our new death, our fresh daylight brought across heather with our voiced grief, our unvoiced desire, our breathing swaying our hearts, these good skies nourished by clean intent and verbal country, our blood climbing out of every possible void. Vista grants entanglement with distance, our ideas winging from marrow to clouds, from moon to teeth, our seed brimstoned straight upward into angels, our eternal destination, every winter heart inventing warmth, sparks from friction light our middle ground, our universe upon this stranded earth, body under thunderous body, melded together. Our crippled symmetry wraps around our homeland, our trees bent toward roofspace, our rivers flowing through our tubs, our sinks, our soil sunk into scientific theory, and bearded babble, our carousing meant to drown us in midday frenzy, our creation reduced to an accident of our clay. Omit what isn't important, and nothing, not even nothing, will be left. Clarify what is obvious by absolving what is strange, the embrace of the less than fashionable by the more than right, our insistence that what we uphold belongs to us, what we denounce belongs to us, what we ignore belongs to us, and all that doesn't belong to us belongs to us, if anything belongs to us. Our transgressions haunt our idle afternoons, our last mornings, diaphanous shame and clanging guilt, sinless but still to blame, shackled by conscience, marred by unawareness, perpetually shaken awake. Rainbow our sheets with puberty and loss, our fluids given to love and surprise, our refractions delivered through light beyond wealth, our promises of treasure hollow, our chromatic legend an unknown glyph mistaken for truth, for standard coding. Separate us into ribbons of tonal inequality, our deep night waking into modal indifference, our verbs as grains of sand thrown into the sea as acknowledgment of our aloneness, inspiration elsewhere, gone spelunking into factual wilderness, leaving us with sameness and comfort, fields of gentle sunshine, skies of consistent solace and watchfulness, regret ugly in dirty yards, boredom alive with value, specialness loaded with context, this merciful meadow of words, bestowed upon the eager and earnest, above cavern and pit and abyss, our deliverance from lightlessness into darkness, purely mined and cut, blackness cored into candid death. Thus begins our belief.

Complex laughter, come to steal our grief, come to tighten our bellies and sway our trees, to instruct us in good mirth, to settle our dust. We behave within the shape of our upbringing, taught to think actions, to verb objects, to respond to anger with transparency, to folly with cheer. Lessons learnt of forests burnt, our votive souls too close to grass in wind, our water buckets full of seed, and every rhyme reasoned into embers, every clause infected with lust. Passion honed for mental substance, the juice of proliferation spilled upon our trust, our evenings given to gentle mining. Tell us to mind and we will agree to attend, our foundation of cooperative sense, our semblance of obeisance, our hands folded in our laps as behaved children, our eyes on the bonfire of teaching, our minds open for pour and stir. Nature educates fool and prodigy, sage and king, not with beauty but with struggle and sequence, those strange and heartrending cycles, death of the egg and the energy of corpses. When we bedtime ourselves, when we tuck our oughts into our nevers, our story told by the lights on our ceiling, our candles flickering with our sighs, we slip into revolving oblivion, our duty to wake refreshed and eager, to labor hard so that we might sleep deep, to enjoy our days as if they were the stuff of dreams. Simple tears come to steal our mirth, come to loosen our will and fell our trees, to train us in sorrow, to scatter our sands. Token us westward into samplers on walls, shadowing armchairs with bearable inadequacy, our wisdom congealed into threaded platitudes. The logical construct is one of elegance, that consistent fraud, our reconciliation with the imperfect and our inability to embrace the chaotic our clear dilemma, the roughly elegant as our compromise. Tell us to rebel and we will stare down destruction, our rootedness and collaborative craze, our simian obstinancy, our symbiont hands clasped against profit and usury, our minds joined. Vilify us in dreams and lament our unattended cautionary tales, our wrecked sand too close to tidal ambition, our ugly crops strangling our handsome weeds. Honesty defeats confusion, and the haphazard rules the head, our steady goal to save us from ourselves. Lessons learnt of cities burnt, our volcanic hearts swelling under drapes, our vases full of unmet eggs, and every reason rhymed to ash, every phrase gray with grit. Weep when weeping is proper, sob when it's sobbing time, cry vigorously throughout the days of crying, and laugh grief away when grief grows stale. Rivery exultation bears our comfort downward toward old surf and shore submission, our leaf boat avoiding dead eddies and impediments, boulders and fallen logs, this lioness current swifting us toward dreaming seas. Our crooked squints lounge upon loins, hammock lessons of fantast and definition, courage to stare, courage to reach for land not ours, the terrain of the other now belonging to our rigorous witness, our crusading differentiation never open to scrutiny. Categories assure us of domain, provide for our antagonism and concord, build knowledge and delude us into unknowing, blind to far peripheries and near severings, our shifting uncertainty stabbing our eyes. Discretion validates care, the diminishment of expanse, the harbinger of family and respect for elders, antiquity as value, wisdom through time, quality as craft and quantity as dubious, our best behavior arisen from constraint, our worst aspects settled into method. Automatic response triggers critical waves, cleverness and adroitness washing away gut feelings, our initial reflex drowned. We avoid the swamps of personal digression, our path along the windswept ridge protected from autoerotic flood, too aloof to ferment. Pleasured bodies writhe within their fortune, their fetishes prevalent, our faiths flown up chimneys and air pipes, our blood pumping brainward, heartfelt, this logical fervor and vibrant sense, our corporeal uncertainty. Liberate us from everything we cherish, from everything we lack, our will to flatten desire into death, or our thoughts of death across desire, freedom as imaginations of achromatic travel, wanderers and intellectuals, stars and children, this migration from rare to nonexistent, from nothing to nothingness, all mean within duty, every twist calibrated and registered, our new ethical machinery ornamented with daisy constraints, floral patterns intent upon soothing the harried mind, peace and assurance for every child of calm, every philosopher of accident, more reverie than analysis, our beloved death. Thus begins our belief.

Rivery exultation through our favorite vale, the sky lowering to water's edge, our wrists wet, our clothes shared, the boulders ours for avoidance, the banks ours for reflection, our hearts not inclined toward the sea nor the heavens, our eyes squinted for white. All evil is light in the eyes of widest time, from the vista of nonchalance to the promontory of utter concern. Altitude hales attitude, the keen scarcity of air, our elevation of spirit, our levitation of will, highest reach and lowest esteem, the comedy of success. Shadowy thrills for the flipped and topsy-turvy, those disappointed in the light and sweetness, those upside-down with doubt and chagrin, the lure of darkness as able contrast to majestic day, the cool spaces of neglect and forgetting. Language stabs our dragons in their soft bellies, wounding them doubly, spilling blood and words. Our union revolves on its axis, the marriage of space and void, inclination and imagination, our passion for chaos piqued by order and colored into feminine time, our belief in the deeper night. Bridesmaid us to dawn, keep us safe for surprise, and gentle us to another night, pulsed side to side by the blood within. Ravel our strands before we merge into browny black, our meaning shrunk into a swatch, a clump of muddy spirit, our contrast lost to mingling, our apologies for the condition of this world. Tote us to the mountaintops where our shinier surfaces gleam, above these venal streets with their flickering boxes, our forgiveness offered to whomever is responsible for this world. Cacophony and static, fit and proper, our choir from the quagmire, suited to mingle and robed to match, our voices jagged to rip mountaintop flags and sails and honeymoon sheets, our clang rather charming. Our magnificence waits. What we are isn't what we will be, our natures as fluid as solid, our unknowing unknowable and diagonal to our scoped horizons, our intrigue situated near our security, all focus false. Creative quietude in our frenetic calm, superior energy and superior rest, the magnetic tug of the impossible path, our fading updraft and our ascending slide, all to kilter us out of kind. Tradition flies out the window when the air is sucked from the room, temple or teepee, privy to salon, as if the reciprocity of interior and exterior exists outside of time, vestibule to copse, oasis to foyer, all in a spaceless dream granted to travelers. Heed our call for play, our lark through hunger and epidemic, the skipping out of formation into frenzy, all disasters shared, naive and welcome, all manic joy pitched beyond hearing. Pond water trembles our limbs, our paramount need rising, our chests strong with air, our raw survival gray and grayer, contrasted for perpetuity, inclined toward unknown sorrowful storms, snow as shepherded cheer for someday seasons, for summery hearts, for us dark-spleened romantics who skinnydip and dive from promontories into swirling basins of tears. Gazing past concern, we utter words meant for skeletal dust, for the keen nuance of elevated will, clausal and ever traveling, mortal and beyond divine, our voices resonant and resilient. Giant contradictions as lullabies for the dead, our vibrations shaking knowledge off its shelves, our sanctioning uncertainty as some condone caution, all for soothing guilt into candy, all for melting snow into semen. Rain shines with coming life, atmospheric sperm falling upon the innocent and the vicious, the resistant and the primed, our earth surviving nicely until its own inevitable apocalypse. Now descends gravity's love to press our flesh to water, to lift our blood to clouds, our peace reliant upon tension, upon forces absolute, the defiant abstractions of colorblind poets, the wishes of lonesome boys and lonelier girls. Our aspirations are cobbled together from childhood scraps, from nostalgia and pillow visions, pajama heat and sleepy trauma, all of our hopes roaming the confines of snowglobes. Dismantled conventions gleam under noon's gaze and sparkle with midnight's favor, dark as too knowable and too dark, ruins always lovelier than structures intact, whatever was not as compelling as what couldn't last, what wouldn't be more beautiful than all that was. Hang us as tapestries, our colors chosen to be servants of differentiation, slaves to beauty, tribes of same, stories shared across time, or coded into veins, hope belonging in patterns, distributed and woven into remembered memory, vast webs of eventual forgetting, tangled into community, insidious and bloated with justification, navel to crypt, satisfaction to horror, our aspirations ill with contagious viruses, wild with aggressive ideas, curiosity inflicted and spotlight afflicted, these leanings regulated by decorum, ornamentation the sleight-of-hand, order the fascination, younger freedom before death. Thus begins our belief.

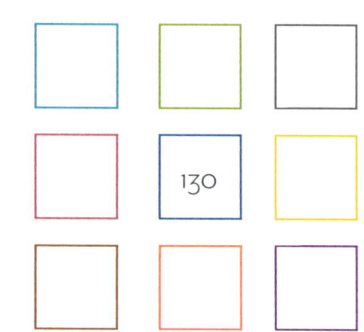

Watery star of our new death, the lap of lake against our time's boat, rising. Light shimmers off our sails, our white sheets of wonder, our day skies free of intent, our chosenness absolute. Shepherds on the beach, our crooks stuck in sand, our sheep lounging upon the whiter shore, our defining star visible in daylight, this covenant of ours with the just promiser, our inventor. Celestial sea of our old life, the wash of rain across our roofspace, settling. Fatherland to homeland, our journey from horror to terror, scissors to documents, curls to cutting wire, empirical harm under our indifferent sun, what we know to be true and what ought to be sacred and what we protect as ours, the holy spaces of history, the archives of suffering, the humor of mistake, all streamed across time as a creation joke, promised land to death chambers, clay to ash, father to judge, our city of light, their cities of ruin, vengeance wrought with bombs of genius and ingenuity. Reeds hide our future captain, our storm navigator, the one with stories that stare across distance and stare down time, perishable and imperishable, our soft-spoken stutterer, our harsh-voiced avenger. To heal isn't to forget, isn't to perform miracles, isn't to transcend. As barterers, we provide fish and bread for ourselves and everyone on our slope, without magic, our skill in gab and scales, haggling justice, this for those and ours forever, our patch of land our birthright, our temples of ash louder than cannons or victory bells, our fathers hearing the original words and the inscrutable lullaby. Take our lives but leave our soil, our identity in our lands, our promised places across the holiest of histories, the ground our corporeal bank, our time treasure and faith foundation, our blood mop. From the well we are lifted into mystery, the lure of elsewhere coves, our exotic hearts seeking our mates, our elsewhere loves. Map our future with a howling past, our seers all touched, every one, madness from proximity to the divine, truth samewise, their prophecy anchored in yesterday's aftertaste. Validate our moral stance with mortal slant, the tasted fruit and the shake of our fists, the bloody sea and gleaming spears, the burning forest and local flood, all for the benefit of resonant telling. Meaningful sounds from our mouths, canted to codify and instruct, to challenge and befuddle, our stars in their perfect places of mischief. Pleasure in bodies and value in spirit, our split focus, our beliefs distributed across panorama as blemish, as mitocondrial drift, our whispers stolen by expanse. Meaningless sounds from our mouths, chanted to scare and bewilder, to dwarf those of us who exist as stars with planet longing. Watery star of our thirst, whiter than purity, staining our trousers as sunlight stains wandering sails, our childhood wonder knobbed into aging hands, those clutching rope and wheel and absolute horizon, those colored with folly and those twisted with poverty, our souls smeared with gratitude. Thoughts worm their way through our borders into our doomed skulls, our egregious doubts infecting future tombs, our promised release from monochrome into spectrum unhappening, our old life never fully washed away. We don't journey from crib to grave without guide, or so we hope, or so we believe, our reason inclined to faith, our faith carried as water, our thirst attractive to bedouins and entrepreneurs, usurers of tragedy and pluck, sellers of triumph destined to perish. Our prophets challenge our kings to verify divine law, our snot-nosed youths endearing and teachable, our hoary-haired elders enriching and unreachable, our masses slain by ignorance and mortared into history, etched as homily into sacred walls, sewn into bands worn around biceps, twice-told forgotten. We motivate ourselves with money and civil duty, our ancestral prods, their mighty influence, their default wisdom and our petty deeds. Scatter our efforts as failures, our failures as sublime debris, our seed as divinely inspired palaver, our platitudes unbearable. We arrange ourselves into schemes, the illusion of distinguishment, our double-staged theater lit to accentuate contradiction, this religious demarcation of role-play, architecture of belief and sensibility, to relegate illicit artists to odalisques, our soliloquies as staccato nonsense, framing confusion with order, territories with walls, all memorial sentiment, nostalgia, paranoia, projection and depression, measuring our dreams with cognitive strategy, actors stealing reality from the audience, lovers thieving sex from the enlightened, our immediate need leveraged by practical concerns, suspended above mystery and mystical seizure, ornate flowering against newest frost and death. Thus begins our belief.

Simple fields of daisies open for our joy, whiter than paramount clouds, early lit and late risen, sacrificial to bees and wolves, tantamount to submission, planted by chance, nourished by system, our observance clean and given. Fake lions gnaw on our bones, given to artificial day as tokens of our substitution, wine into blood, blood into oil, our marrow good for regal manes, for straight and gleaming teeth, our flesh gone to dust before our skeletal faiths. Pattern nuance cries for icon, pentagram and tomb, across and afire, stone crusade and brimstone angels, the glory of contrast and the universal stew, our stone rolled into traffic, into the straightening and narrowed path. Pavement swept for winter sun, the clear heavens and the chapel afternoons, our melancholy lit by empty time, our crayons and marbles shared. Core and mantle, apple and hearth, knowledge and ease stunting our growing love, our unconditional flurry of affection for the fortunate and able. Follow us into flames and resolute purity, our swords stained with virgin sweat, our shields forged with universal restraint, our helmets agleam with divine approval, soldiers for our mother. Bleed across our linen, this special cloth of false memory, our nakedness wrapped in the illusion of duration, our white story colored with the dreams of wandering children. Hands folded in prayer or clenched at flanks or shoved into pockets seldom stop tanks. Hands gripping pens or rockets or breasts never stop hurricanes, carnal linguists drowning as easily as sons of preachers, our loins as bombs in our nether homes, pleasure as heat from our world's core. Grace corrupts denial, our belief in our measured worth falling under our inherent value, our love of bootstrapping tempered by our salvation lust, our big love made small. We canyon our prayers into grand spectacles to awe ourselves as children, the hush of depths beyond sight and the far blackness unlistenable. Fake lambs bleed upon our bones, hidden from genuine wolves as proof of our sacrifice, sperm into hood, mood into foul, our fleece good for legal theft, for bent and grimy shoulders, our skin exposed to air before our shy creator. To the least of these we fail to give unassailable haven, our love unhumbled, our pride unstrung, our violence in our fibre, in our pulse and visions of paradise, in our ultimatums and destiny. Hands fold paper into dolls who spill their wistfulness into our margins, our seams leaking imagined life, our gutters flowing with arterial energy, our sewer hearts eager for the rush. Unconditional love would burn a hole through our world, if it existed, if it could be more than imagined. Our seduction of the imperative and our translation of the kind redeem us from our oldest quandary to our youngest quaverings. Everlasting waves of laughter lap against our timely swoon, our spirits plummeting into tangled roots, our hair still wrapped in trees, our laundered sheets creating sun, this system of observance and objective action, fake wilderness in our boots. All evil gnaws at token time, crucified for substitute sheep, everything raised for global enjoyment, afternoon delight and sticky stretch, lovers swept away lowest to highest, pavement to steeple, the newest now clearing away the next rhyme, every serious reason piled upon our faith like stones. Terror finds us wherever we congregate and wherever we don't, our fear of our darker selves, that tedious dread, that cogent refrain, our need to sequester ourselves in velvet pews and red letter motel testaments, our desire to be frightened but not afraid. Send for us today when nothing is happening, when everything is wrong, and we will provide escape or purpose, diversion or death, our affection spread across everything awkward, everything disappearing. Crenellate our moral yard, protection against neighboring confusion and certainty, our natural realm, our supernatural world, spiked walls and lawn mines, coded texts and pearly traps. Our lives matriculate via salvation, our acceptance of a knock and a promise, the advancement of a weaponless army, soldiers with souls away from home. Marginal visionaries and conventional rulers fade rapidly into murk and controllable side effects, placebo messiahs for the scientific masses, our true foundation in the most logical sense, before our ascensions out of supreme love above all of our giant steps and favorite things. Categorize us into cordate expressions, not rigid strips of logical language, our sanctuary of true emotion and irony, our hearts given to singular accomplishment and those who honor great failure, our love flown above despair, rigor and facetious banter, our play serious and elusive and redemptive, our effort born from ferocious ambition, set to ravage the adventurous select, primed to annoy the cautious elect, breathless and relentless, more lyrical than esoteric, our future unfolding as glorious wrong, as victory and death. Thus begins our belief.

Summerlong burn brought to bear upon our backs, our freckles dark, our tongues fresh with spite, our spines knobbed as tree roots, the sun neither our creation nor our creator, our childless father not a star but the maker of stars, our mother unknown. Desert home and eastward gaze, the sunrise in our bloodstream, the heat in our words, our voices raised together, our prophecy global and resonant, the dunes piled upon our passions, our deaths piled upon our deaths, our newest revenge taut and bawdy, our future eternal. We exist to worship origin and destination, our nows caught and flared with quickening energy, the present obsolete before enjoyed, melded out of next into never. Concession steals fortitude, unless bargained with brilliance, and we are shrewder than they are blessed, we are bolder than their confidence or their righteous swagger. Glamour haunts our periphery, reservoir to quarry, knob to gulch, everything glittering and tangled, all that is wild and seen. When we glow we light the mountainside, our laughter as children echoing off the cliffs as oblation chimes, our strength as a multitude shaking the whole world. Come stand us in good stead, our violence as pure as wind, our meditation better guidance than landmarks, our refined honor the talk of the industry. Gone are the days of autonomy and struggle, the bliss of uncertainty. We know the walls are thickest where it counts most. Cluster wonder into pouches warm, sharpen virgin swords on old infidels, deliver peace with austerity and justified slaughter, and may prophecy be kind to our sons and daughters. Gone are the days of concession and compromise, the agony of status quo. We know the fields are sweeter beyond those hills. Bury our hatchets in totems wise, our elders petrified into leafing stone, our individuality deliberate and good, our best hope for maturing, our body of knowledge a lusty boy. Raise our empathy to stab our doubts and those monsters who resist our persuasions, our frail wishes ill widows, our deaths all maiden voyages. Our left hands claw at heaven, filthy from cleansing, the sinister wink and the flicked spark, our protocol in flames, our devotions met with ridicule, chased into harsh lands as pigs from royal surgery. Our differences are acknowledged across this tapestry, subtlety and broad swipe, the sweep of nuance, the sting of clarity, our territorial insistence honed for sharpest hurt. Our similarities show in our bloodstreams, translucent and subterranean, the span of circulation, the prick of peer, our proprietary gush, our shared coagulation. Youth is prey and protectorate, nature's survival instinct, our lurid cache as innocence luring plunder, as temptation to persist, the perseverance of supple time in awkward limbs, in virulent hearts. Simple fields of freckles on a favorite narrowing back, sacrificed for a tight belly and childless power, the behavior of the uninstructed, open to attack, our stingers poised, our transparent motives becoming probable ease, nonchalant and effective, our learning burnt into our bowels and lungs, our children sunk into votive oil. Attitude scorches tongues suited for regal minds and ribs exposed to desert gaze, our devouring of confidences, our renouncing pattern for passion, energy for blood, the levitated icons of our fathers reaching empty status, profane images unseen. Action begets reaction, domino to death, our illegal crescendo and climactic flourish, the politics of skin and maidenly organs, stallion gifts for pendulum eros and egos, our swings westward into secular obscenity. We lobby for control of black blood, our lands fertile with unrefined death, our skies empty of stars, the flow of anger outward not upward, our blades cutting skyscrapers down to tents, our words making oases where there were none before, where our enemies will find no haven. Unflinching fidelity tribes the herd, restorative, dangerous, galvanizing, our children future steel. We migrate across territories not belonging to us, not belonging to anyone, land as repository and plunder, terrain unnoticed for its luminescent skin. Absent us with peril, our disappearance marked by void as if vacuums weren't abhorred, as if erasures weren't mere mistakes disguised as intention, our killings justifiable, our living likewise. We conform to protocol to survive, the establishment of rules and the designation of punishment, our ancestral mores unshaken by undone time, strangers in proximity, our cloistered guidance of absolutes, our willingness to progress, resistance against fashionable solutions of expediency further securing our treasure against outsiders, our legitimate arrogance, forever and always strongest when isolated within traditional boundaries, repetitious and affirming to every willing soul, all of the faithful, our family growing, substance and spirit, sacred and scarce and scared, yearning toward resolve more than resolution, distance calculated as fear more than respect, our dreaded death. Thus begins our belief.

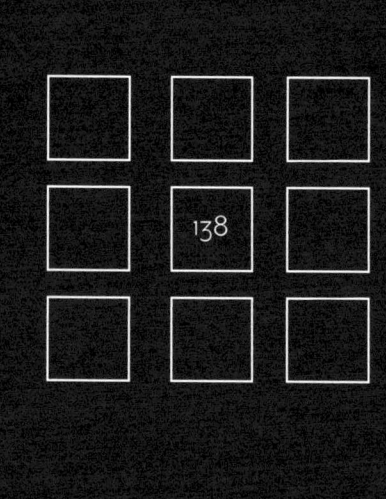

belief, what begins as doubt, death around life, now and again now, goes back to doubt, doubt as faith without fulfillment, longing without proof, the corrosive guilt from caging uncertainty, and uncertainty caged, for those who would try to shield certainty, to protect it from sharp inquiry, becomes the uncontainable beast, the great destroyer, whereas uncertainty left to roam takes only occasional prey, what it needs to survive, the young or weak, the foolish or wayward, and nature's discordant harmony is sustained, the fit and the lucky confident with unknowing, what can't be known or won't ever be known, the unknowable different than the uncertain, the unknowable dependent upon the knowable, the uncertain dependent upon the certain, the certain nothing without its negative, or not its negative but its shadow, or not its shadow but its reflexive creator, its delineator, all things known by their opposites or shifting edges, their connections, such as faith to doubt and doubt to logic, faith not succumbing to logic because logic is an intellectual faith requiring belief in language, this system built upon signs or symbols or sounds, this notion of sequence, of what follows, such as belief following doubt and doubt following belief, or spinning in parallel, faith and belief as neighboring spokes, one thing leading to another, hub to rim, rim to hub, everything leading to everything else, all in proper order or all properly ordered, structure and form rising from energy, energy emerging from formlessness as form, again and again or once forever, forever as a word of faith and not belief, belief as a word more closely aligned to doubt than faith, faith born of sinew and belief of synapse, or not of synapse but of cellular division, or not of sinew but of sweat, this physical doubt, this great greatness deconstructing arrogance without killing pride, without burning dignity to ash, or if to ash then not oblivion, oblivion a word not of doubt but of belief and defeat, defeat a word of faithlessness and not of disbelief, disbelief the beginning of living faithfulness, of generative cheer. Belief abides with fools on thrones and disbelief with kings on battlefields, or not just with kings but within all hearts in conflict, or all hearts royal or ordained or beastly or outcast, coronated or feral or mistaken or martyred, those pounding for vengeance or those fluttering with faint expectations, their faintest trust in cleansing doubt, or if not cleansing then revitalizing vitality inhaling doubt and exhaling faith, doubt's necessary waste, not as toxins but as belief's antidote, anti and un and dis as crucial elements, or if not necessary, welcome, linguistic brooms to clear the streets of clumped confetti, or if not colored paper suns, stale joy. Doubt, shed by belief, life throughout death, leaf-fall and leaf-fallen and falling now, is uplifted by air in turmoil, doubt as fulfilling faith, the proof of longing, chaotic certainties as organisms of change. Or—and this is a galvanizing or—orderly uncertainty vivifies creation. Or—and this is an or as true as false—belief is death and death is not to be believed, not amid transmutable eternity, not within spiritual objects. Art, despite its human stamp, can be volcanic, cellular, celestial. Belief should equal or exceed art. Art, whenever and wherever it surfaces, as reconstituted nature or projected dream, can be as false as true. Belief can build fortunes of power, and rule for centuries unto millennia. Art is too seldom the destroying angel. Belief must be willing to die for faith. Faith ladders art to the heights of knowing doubt. Art doubts art and faith disbelieves death. Death won't shrink from art or faith or belief or life, only time, or if not time, its shadow, timelessness, or if not its shadow, its own creating light. Thus begins everything, the death-inclined and the beyond-death-inclined, what is made and what is unmade and what was never made at all. Then, action. Then, making follows being. Then magma, division, and vastness soon incomprehensible. The unsilenced imagination in river and bloodstream, in nebula and dream, the parasite contains its host, motion is separate from meaning and belief is secondary unto superfluous, or if not superfluous, non-essential, essential as in essence, essence as in sense and senselessness, the thing and the space of the thing, the word said and the word thought of before said, all mused madness across world history, all cross-cutting and time severances, all flung leaves and each battered heart and every enigma, what becomes of partial wisdom of temporary conversion, shift into change into the ever-decomposing new, belief frantic or smug around disappointment, or a

not disappointment, disillusionment, or if not smug, condescending, the privilege of the non-despairing, those who have stopped answering whenever doubt comes calling, or if not doubt, faith, its winsome cousin, all mused madness throughout world memory, all earnest defiance of settling and stratification, in fever and cluster and circulation and sea. The beginning won't suffice and the ending isn't telling, is unavoidable, won't shard. Words go unsaid and words get forgotten and words twist and act as made being. Erupt. Develop. Undarken. Out of the reaching and destructive light came everything, all that is known or knowable or known to be unknown or unknowable, all that is urged into growth and brought to fated ruin, all manifestations of naive progress, the cycling cataclysms, the reinvented tombs, bones as pencils and marrow-made words scrawled across thresholds and portals, erased with blood, blood-recited and blood-requited and heart-soaked, memory flooded with emotive drought, out of that original anonymity, the creator of creating, the shattered silence, the reformulated hush, the sudden luxury of forgetfulness, or if not forgetfulness, incomplete remembrance, the chronic unnegotiable need for mystery relegating complete completeness to the corner of theoretical whimsy, the largeness of mind and the potential for soul immeasurable, or if not immeasurable, not to be self-quantified, not to be intruded upon, not by other or maker or anyone of unmystifying ego, this darkness-breathing marvel of made, these worlds of observable energy, or if not observable, apprehensible, or if not apprehensible, imaginable, coarse-grained imagined and loved into exquisite relief, loved as revelatory, adored as perpetually revealing, that reaching and destroying light. The collision of matter is thought-resultant. The existence of matter is nomenclature. Or—and this is a monumental and mischievous or—if not named out of love, loved because named, loved because naming is specific, met and unmet, not captured or categorized, not limiting or unlimited, but witnessed and rewitnessed, rain-gathered and windswept, immolated and egg-shocked, sworn-swirled through and around time, or if not time itself, its imagined substitute, its blinding sheen, its lust-inducing momentous wink, or if not its glance, its stare, its compounding attentiveness, the affection of sky upon bodies of water. Loneliness, arisen from peerlessness, discovered its apotheosis in unrecognized love, or if not love, if unknown as love, what is said to be hand-wringingly unseen, not being seen as commensurate with not being loved, even if being loved isn't equivalent to being seen, equivalence as slipshod nomenclature, naming as neither pre- nor post-creative, pre or post as immediately approximal, eternally wrong, or if not eternal, annoyingly resistant to change, change as chance made holy. Culture rots as affectation and rot becomes loam and loam is the dark home of nourishing will, will sprung not from instinct or code or wiring but as reaction to mortifying constancy, this inaccurate verbing, this nouned inadequacy, this renowned ache, this reknowable and ever-renewable desolation of spirit. Rain gathers and wind sweeps and the mind is portent-wobbled and sameness-stunned. Or—and this is an or of bemusement—the mind climbs beyond its rooflines into overcast thought, into cognitive sightlessness, the unavailable vista. If cause is self-satisfying and effects are self-satisfied, if the goat seeks pleasure from the sheep and the sheep from the serpent, if fire purifies milk and leaves claim ascendency, if hinges swing toward spherical glory and abstraction codifies loss while sparkling grief, answers reside in confusion, truth crouches in the dust, or if not truth, some semblance of seem, the seemliness of soil, the seamlessness of space, the seeming dissolution of translucent nonsense, the sensate force of flesh upon flesh, body of water upon body of water, breath on throat, pulse in belly, the stomach for mess and legs for the distance, corporeal majesty and mortal muck, the transparent throb, this transcendent lilt, or if not rarified, real, and if not reality, chosen, choice as a version of foundation, of solid footing, of adaptive grace. Thinking reels out of thought's bed toward faith's escarpment, shoeless and rumpled and coatless and flawed, believed into motion by natural law, stumbling not on meaninglessness but on meaning, or if not meaning then on meaning's echoes, or if not meaning at all then on the debris of meaningless resolution, the urge to fall upward unorigined, not that leaf-in-updraft fantasy, not some carnival child's

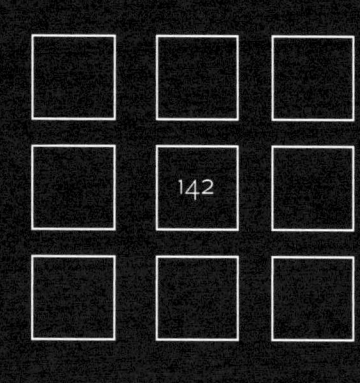

balloon tragedy, not those unglued feathers of myth or that blazing chariot bound for virginal comfort, all fine as tales but hardened as telling, telling as bloodflow, listening as waterous absolution, water-rise and waterdrop and bloodloss, forgiving the bloodless and the careless and the cutting edge, the careful and the bloodletters and the newly stained, the trenchant and the too-nuanced and the sanctum-shrugged, the cowardice of the genuinely frightened, the intransigence of the knee-buckled, forgiveness as cloudburst, or if not storm-delivered then lungsure, moisture as atomic and uncollected, or if gathered then noncongregational, unionized neither as specialists nor factotums, snowflakes as miraculous independence, every mind a contracted laborer, the choiring soloist, the rustled leaf, the rustling leaf, the good-gone unstemmed necessity. Then comes the muddling hand-holding mass of beauty assassins, of wonder pimps and cleverness whores, assay-nodded and viscera-robbed, bleary-eyed and hateful and forgiven, or if not forgiven, forgiving and forgiveable, or if not nimbly relative, if not endlessly availed, then ridiculous, selective and selected, those selection processes sealed with coagulated assurance, dismissive poverty to hospitable wealth, grease in the bowels, boulevards in the brain, all lined with sensible stepping-stone craft, suburban malaria, ancestral gifts delivered by strangers, jingled wiith persuasion, smiled with unwavering loathing for subtlety. Contradict. Mystify. Self-deprecate. Distrust the vulnerable and the invulnerable and the smug and the witty and the clodheaded and the brackish and the elitist and the earnest and the distrustful. Or, unequivocally, trust everyone, be everywhere. Then again, melancholia-steeped with unregrettable longing, after one canted instant of unrepeatable hope, words fail. Speech produced the unmattering universe. Up from the loins rushes acidic youth. The sanctuary of thought is petrified with method. All ushers fear inexplicable duplication. Concur. Clarify. Self-adulate. The world's medications will fill its cracks and basins and depressions and rifts. See the pocks shallow and shallower. Watch canyons and vales testify to strata and be sentenced to prescriptions of sedimental conviction. Language accrues and its sentences are its conduits. Here comes clogging silence. Or, most assuredly, if not silence, its tidier cousin, hush, or if not tidier, aggressively shorn, or if not tiresomely metaphorical, just less silent. Refuse all exclusionary toasts to life's lesser cousins. Refuse belief without faith and faith without doubt and doubt without humility. Or—and this is a taunting or, or if not taunting, goading, or if not goading, proselytized, or if not postulated, suggested—trust everywhere, be everyone. Then again, sing death to sleep and flee all dawnings. Unplotted history nags creation, buzzes about the gods, lays its eggs in carrion and waste and outlasts civilization. Evolutionary vines strangle the town statue. Devolvement is fallacy. Blue planets aren't collectible. In the margins of mind hovers the thought that men can but proceed from what they know, a procession of literary jokers and lummoxes, of poseurs and middling saints, those central to fools' errands and those placebo messengers, those telegrams of obligatory make-believe, those prophets of mere propositions, all stiff on the main drag, all dressed in tomorrow's ridicule while side-yard weeds bloom for solitary children as the company of mind. Then again, wistful and nostalgia-sodden, with irreversible fondness, after chords of indefatigable harmony, words fail. Discuss. Codify. Self-modulate. Now as nearness never comes nearer, now as arrival grows into myth or delusion or antiquated concept, or if not out of fashion then out of step, this march toward oblivion, this refusal to admit defeat, or if not defeat, endemic stalemate, or if not a game, pretense, this verbal soldiering, these analogical conventions prone to tedium and the poor sort of excess, tradition as laudable constraint, the bursar as shaman, the librarian as witch, this hardware of soft-portent, polished beyond gleam and dented beyond good-as-new smoothing, now that the nearness of nearness comes without nearness to itself, the far edge of nearness circling to the rear while the far edge of faith eddies until stagnant, pools until dry. Then neglect unto madness, of if not neglect, spotlight, and madness assured, or if not madness, complaisance, and if not jadedness, artistic professionalism, conception to irony to inviolate eroticism, or if not pleasure, critical relief, or if not intelligent synthesis, curious

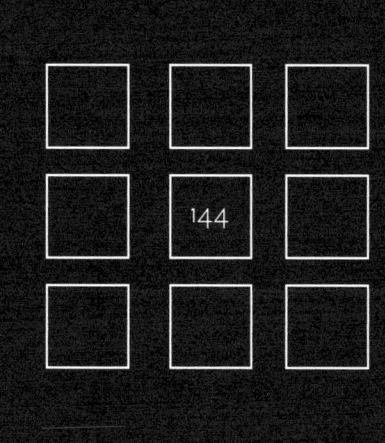

design, spurt to flow, gush to joy, piety to impotence, salutory perpetuation, statutory agape, beast to angel, bitch to cur, mutts in pockets and ditches in church, the janitor in the organist and the priest in the grail, rabbi or sheik or roshi or clown, the gargantuan codpiece or the chastity thread, or if not sensual, consensual, and if not clubby, collective, and if not communal, passionate, and if not private, singular, and if not godly, goodly, in full and effervescent devotion, or if not full then nearer to full than not, this empty grunt and grind of entertainment in front of wholeness shunned, or it not whole, multivariate, or if not sufficiently complex, territorially satisfying, the satisfaction of local challenge, the sustained gasp, the shrift of long-living, the neat trick of contentment, that faultline syntax for stiffen and thrust, for lift and collapse, for engendering technique in an engendered species, or if not for everyone, for individual hearts everywhere. Sequence gives way to whim and whim conforms to precedent and structure alludes to principle and the patterns of chromatic energy swirl in the margins and curl in the mess. Gesture elucidates intent and planning incites revolt and accident mirrors experience. Beware of condescending frameworks. Stay suspicious of rhetorical flurry. Prefer telling to told. Climb into storybeds with animal prowess and wake with steward acuity, the refinement of perception, the burden of discernment, the freedom of errata, the tenacity of trust. Stars and cockroaches aren't impressed by stained glass or prosody, gold domes or intricate weaves. Make. Rarify. Self-advocate. Time turns to end this, to say goodbye to semenizing and lactose posturing, to spend aggression on wonder and not enlistment, to let the disappointing day diminish into a recovery evening, to allow the night to tumble attic to cellar, to fail to convince the self of sanctity or sinfulness. Worth is as mercurial as any mental weather. Suffering isn't pervasive or it wouldn't be suffering—it would be the state of things. The state of things isn't all that is the case but more reasonably all that isn't, the unknown as relevant as the known and the unknown as the haystack to the known's needle, a haystack of needles, a haystack of resemblance in a wide field of semblant haystacks. There is no finality in seem, so let be be what it wishes to be or must become and leave it alone until it visits. Belief, with its meaty hands, kills while the innocent sleep and keeps on killing in zenith daylight. Doubt kills, too, but passively, with attendent empathy. Faith knows it shouldn't kill but all too often is just following belief's orders. Nature kills efficiently and art kills stupidly by its own hand, death not hanging around to hear art's will or colorless testament read aloud to red-eyed family. Death's veil is the conception of belief, that oppressive need to fabricate a passible portrait of the unknown, the emotive likeness of an interior phantom. Points of view are infinite, if extra-human. If distinctly homo sapien, they're billions, might never see trillion, might never cohere into a blueprint of universal architecture, can't be harmonized into operatic grandeur, or have always been harmonized far beyond operatic reach or haiku concision, can't be delegated to a stack of language, to any mountain of thought, to any pebble of genius. Art must outcrop and bedrock and pulverize its tradition to understand itself. Not again, not now again, this stridency of artful shoulds, this inductive streaming, this vocative dodge and declarative hammer, these allusional sweets and relentless sourings, this deliberate tangling of platitudes and insights, these reconstituted thoughts recontextualized for approval, or if not approval, applause, or if not intimidation, intimacy, the maker unmasked, the bride unveiled, these ordinary tropes, these extraordinary knots, these cascading clauses of exploratory appeal, all as attenuation and all for naught, these praisings and appraisals, these reactionary doubts, wadded and tossed and unwadded and preserved, iterated and offset, reworked and disremembered, the exemplary condition of morning and the rigor of deep afternoon told in wide-night templates, cross-oriented and cross-dignified, watered down and water-bright, mourned and elegied for metaphorical clout, for tender absurdity, self-serving and self-flagellent, the peck of the executioner, the slobber of childhood fidelity, midlife drift and unconscionable indecision, all intended to cajole and impress and seduce and elicit, this extraction of sympathy, this glint-in-the-eye self-congratulatory ramble, this illicit mantra, this stiff-arming weave and sprint toward time-ending

triumph, toward the clock-stopping frenzy of celebration and heartbreak, the moment-to-moment deftness of excluded absolutes in favor of pantry muse, sounds upon words upon entrenchments and vertigos, daddy's sperm to mommy's milk, a world-faith cross-stitch of the probable and possible, unlikelihoods and tautologies, inklings and inclinations, unhistorical and interpretive, anthropological and scaled to fit, the kiss of the gravedigger and the coo of the wetnurse, these actions witnessed and dreamt and unnavigated and crayoned, automatic flight and deliberated stay, phenomenal and handicapped, sophomoric and spinal, forested with dogmas and wastelanded with whatevers, this deliberate shroud and unautomated shredding, fret to hollow, valise to cupped hands, palm-fronded and oil-washed, work-bent and lotus-calm, sun-prone and bomb-strapped, burning-bushed and ash-fetished, wind-free and wine-staggered, deducible and reducible and obliterative and wrong, partial and connected and elective and sure, stone-idoled and navel-shrined, hip-paradoxed and ephemeral, this human dilemma of egalitarian excess, this smorgasbord of lack, the impropriety of policy and the irresponsible willy-nilly, across the board, around the globe, this universal network of corpuscles and ideas, this private pulse in this one consciousness, all as it is and all as it seems and all as any deem it ought to be, leaf to thaw, sprout to harvest, integral nature infused with the plain and the inscrutable, the logical and the lyrical, seed to flake, bloom to frost, melt to meld, the pondered hand and the mirrored neurons, aspiration and expiration, swollen labia and retracted scrotum, chill and ooze and wilt and crumble, clang and give and take and spurn, adamance and insolence and reticence and shame, affluence and indolence and redolence and pride, this human domain, this centric province, homo charismatic and sapiens ascendent, here in the heartime, all in the meantime, classicist to modernist, agrarian to industrial, flathead to paleface, orthodoxy to reformation, rehearsal to coda to encore, wound to bandage to scar, temperament to action, accusation to execution, this gravity-bound coast to a stop or to a near stop, this going on and these goings on and the eventual cessation, inevitable and gradual, cancerous or morbid, or if not gradual, sudden, fated or unchosen, static to quietude, program to static, this confluence of code and genetic luck, this privileged stigma, this entitlement astigmatism, this omniscient whimsy of ignorant claustrophobia, this grand illusion, brutal and vital and viral and broad, crass and bold and insidious and crude, this linguistic foppery, this suffocating press, this well-hung vocabulist, shoes mismatched and legs a-dangle, once lean with trust and now hope-bloated, or not now again, not now in this symphonic crescendo, this volcanic grotesqueness and cellular accretion, this celestial skit, this scribble-sobbing of whelm and gratitude, this incensed apostasy, this fouled flowering, all the trampling elephants and the quick-jawed termites, associational blather or correlational competence, or the scrabbling genius of almost, a demi-god of manifold approximation, voiced for the long ago and the never ever, here to rape the ill-conceived plastic daughterland, to ensure deeper-voiced sonhood perks and takes notice, the timpanis rumbling and the violins sawing while an orphaned viola squeals her indignation as one tight oboe reeds its superiority. Or—and this is a show-stopping or—a lone accordianist contracts and expands the apocalypse. When is enough enough, enough for a flood or a rapture, a valentine or a matriculation, a whipping or a ruinous kiss, a dressing-down or an undressing or a good talking to, a caress or a grope, or if not a grope, a fond meaty pat, or if not fond, needy, or if not needy, sick, or if not sick, sickening, and the older testament descends and clutches the nape and shoves the visage into a brick wall and the newer testament recoils and pleads for peace in the bloody aftermath, and all of this over a fond meaty pat, an awkward anecdote of expression, a transgressive gesture out of a wilderness of one, not infidelity or debauchery or perversity or elitism, not brimstone-invoking heresy, not crucifixion-deserving clarity, not indiscretion or travesty or snobbery or whine, not exclusivity or hypocrisy or bravura or spin, this fabric of situational use, whatever circumstance asks it to be, blanket or robe or cape or shroud, windbreak or altar cloth or tapestry or noose, smoke-signaler or sail or magic carpet or flag, this unstoppable trundling, this diarrhea of an aesthete, thrust

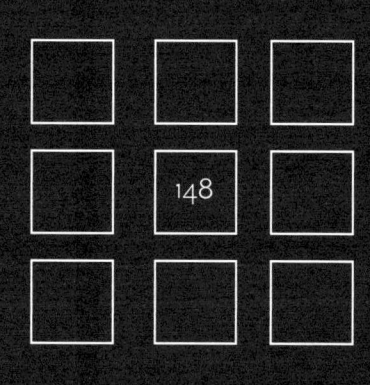

and throb, chug and whirr, this unstemmable ivory tide, roil and surge, undermine and expose, the exposure of an introvert, or if not an introvert, a shy guy, a waters-run-deep gentleman, a product of suburban church-going lineage, an epic-trawling social misfit, this brave chalker, this bold beast of brain, this clever fellow, too clever and not so clever, this sanctification back-slider, pronoun side-stepper, tiptoeing humanist, clumsy-tongued misanthrope, retro-sexist stooge, this triangle-tinging percussionist in the world's most bored national orchestra, this idiot, this blossom, this ungrateful mite, this happy boy, this eager beaver, this strand of drool, this puddle of liquid sky, this expanse of soul, this peripheral scrawler, or if not scrawler, writer, or if not writer, unclassifiable laborer in a clerkhouse of half-mustered resentment, the lovely filigreed workmanship adorning the structure's facade no excuse for its ramshackle interior, its unpopulated rooms, its directionless corridors, its bare cupboards and tasking library, its veiny floorboards and sugar-stench, this house the gentry readily ignore and the hoi polloi see right through, its furnace sound, its chimney tall, its antenna bent and rusty in this cabled world, amid these satellited neighborhoods, or if not neighborhoods, blocks and blocks of block houses, or if not houses, homes, this humanist's reduxe, this fatalist's consolation, these lives unlike any lives, like all lives, authentic and present, undeniable and real, or so it could be shown to any observer, to this anti-hyperbolist, this hairshirter, this bleeding-heart liberal, or if not bleeding, slightly rashed, or if not activistic, apathetic, or if not mamby-pamby, weary with independent cowardice, or if not freeze-frame frightened then big vista numb, this fanfared commoner, this ease-faring conscience, all estuaries and canals with oceanic daydreams, this mule, this stallion, this poets' donkey, this scholars' centaur, or if not centaur, satyr, this closet believer, this pedastal mute, this circus-master mumble and side-show yawn, this captains' wheelhouse lackey circumnavigating chagrin, now that the lie of scale is on the reel, now that the line is taut and the spine is strained, this life and death struggle for soul, or if not soul, intact being, or if not being, becoming, this famished commencement, this insatiable casting about, this boyish lurch and flail, or if not masculine, young, or if not young, oddly innocent, these glitchy speech patterns legitimate, or if bastard, conceived from love, or if not love, loving, ram to ewe, systemic and organic and contrivance and ploy, mammalian and reptilian and avian and insectoid, or if not these, elemental and quirky, marginal and specious, skeptical, not cynical, romantic, not pedantic, angles acute and obtuse, terrain magnified and reconnoitered, landscape crimped and torn, the shenanigans of the freckled kid next door, the wrath of the destroying creator, the magnetic energies of equinox weather and solstice purity, this mind's twister, the mind of a prayerful bag of bones, a shoebox of ash, the elusive or resonant memory of a small gang of saints, this bimbo prophet with janitorial skills, with an organist's resonance, this false modester, this next door trickster, quasi-kind and pseudo-funny, this imagined self, this valed spirit, this nothing close to a bottomless pit, running on toward a fitting end, a galloping palomino toward a milkwood tavern, unraged and quenched, or if still thirsty, not parched, not paradigmed to drown, not narrating as unreliably as that, not again, not on this watch. Or—and this is an or of thundering ifness—if gratitude walks with thieves, if the voice doing the telling is a breaker of trees or a betrayer of clouds, if magnificence is pimped and exulatation is sold down the river, if clay shoes are hobnailed to stomp on daisies, if a paradox-favoring idealist can wave away the everlasting, let death petrify the tongue and putrify the mind, let the brow implode in disgrace, let love leave it void, let sonship ply fresher waters, let bile brim and flow and saturate the keep, let the heart atrophy and stick in a scavenger's gullet, not from the abandonment of belief or even faith, not from the fickle mishandling of grace, but from the egregious lack of trust in awareness, instinctual and intuitive and inherited and earned, these days when awareness is rolled as a drunk or mugged as a spinster, its marriage to meaning annulled, its trousers bunched around its ankles, the awareness of self and the awareness of the one self and the awareness of all selves, the admittance of misunderstanding and the limitless torque of lousy excuses, the allowance for stress and torch-bearing delusion, or not delusion

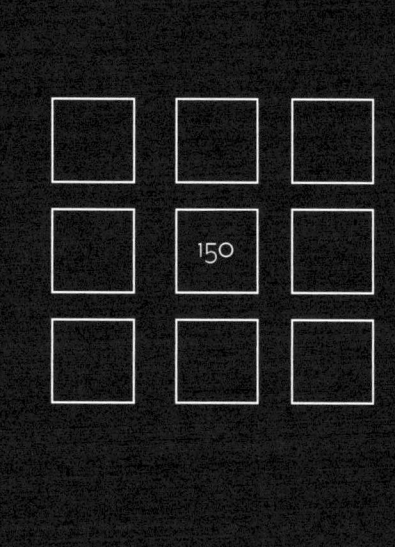

but self-denial, or not excuses but self-panderings, the whitest lies smoldering the longest, now that awareness is pariah, of if not entirely an untouchable, banned from clubs nevertheless, from the halls of secondary concerns and tertiary rooster-strut, from statehouse to townhouse to warehouse to desk, or if not awareness, active witness, that keen celebration of vivid unknowing, not disheartening but enlightening, not dark-age arrogance but the radiance of lilt, that choice of choices, or if not choice, luminous gift, granted to a wandering warbler, or if not wandering, tilted with wanderlust, neither songsmith nor minstrel nor troubador, and if not a warbler then a treetop, rustle and bend, aspirate and sway, a waystation for warbling, for hoot and caw, tweet and trill, self-humming what isn't heard as language, some dispensation of sound, information as energy, this worrisome neglect, this freedom from ambition, or if not freedom, a level accounting, or if not level, not tilted with lust, not stiff with attention, not lachrymose from envy, or if not envy, confusion, not the good confusion but the bad confusion, the devil's stroke, the sensual spokes of that desired hub, the posh still point, the ladled gravy, the iris honey, the vaginal stew, the dandelion blown, the pierced jewels, the borrowed juice, the bartered turn, the cluttered wrists, the braided tongue, the linen lips, the frosted take, the ridden flex, all for the better smith, the good-timing joe, the absolute talent or the pure of heart, the prince with curls or the papa with measure, the snowy lush or the irrepressible letch, the belle of the garden or the insured bricklayer of chaos, the earlier wreck or the latest pout, all in the queue before this watery star, this division cell, this molten pond, this complex joke of risen failure, this polyphonic folly, here in the unfaithing air, here in this unsettled dust, this unsettling residual grief, or if not grief for the spectrum then nostalgia for the array, the once knowing and the need to once not know, this rain-wrapped life, this trailer-park vulnerability, this place where no amount of hunkering or tinkering will save one from capricious selection, where reluctant messiahs are powerless to wave away the cruel or the everlasting, this brutal scourge of confessional leisure, this punctured lung of language, these buried-alive scratchings from a common grave, this shout of compliance, this defiant marathon, this carrion-comfort, this apparatus of flailing precision powered by phosphorescent trust, by stratospheric pressures of delivered chance, while competent death, that paragon of true professionalism, that consummate team player, comes through again and again on its promise of deliverance, its trustable regimen of how to prepare for a day's work, how to get the job done right, with confident and time-honored patience, with reliable tools adaptive to the situation, with ultimate faith in outcome, even in the midst of frustrating all-thumbs hilarity, this double-thumbed telling, opposed to its own elegant touch as well as its embarassing purge and slouch, its seasonal slumps and streaks, the curse of self-forgiveness and the gift of self-admonishment, this grabbing of the gills, this lighting of the heels, this cant of won't and will, this chanting mishap, this fortuitous wrong turn, this banter, this oratorio, these sweet nothings, this sweated something, this gesture of disbelief, this gauntlet of stabbing faiths, this order of magnitude and calculated insanity, this homage to persevering doubt and the grim steed it rode in on, this dissipating storm, this spew of mind, unlike any mind, just like every mind along the way, this way of impossible dreams and heroic stands and probably nots, of almost-certainly-will-never-happens, of what-the-hell-were-you-thinkings, of masterpieces and evil failures of presumptuous reach and of run-of-the-mills, of private destructions and public humiliations, of eviscerated love and steadfast lusts for more and yet more and again now more than more, of self-disciplined enoughs but not more than enoughs, of advocacy gone awry, of advocacy unshown on radar that must be seen from the ground, this way of spit and polish, of salt over the shoulder, of noses to the grindstone and eyes on the prize, of a wing and a prayer and of constant sorrow, of museumed quixotic mayhem, of landmined apologetic invitations to participate in group absolution, this way of belief-mongers and redemptive brutes and poisonous flower girls, of redrafts and mulligans and do-overs, of revolutions and restorations and coups that penetrate to the heart of the matter and come out smelling of no way and the one and only way and every way, this way of ending endlessly.

SURPRISAL

I'm aware of gulfs between theory and
as incontrovertible, won't cross over to
dubbed nor subtitled—let it not fall to
as creation revivify my thoughts and
of wend and scurl and bend—let it
My failure to sing along shouldn't
god, a brash minor angel primed to
to lattice contrasting edges and not
though it is, placed to absorb the
into the world, quite unwilling to
to individually ascend above the
of stray shine, grown not to seduce
to say only what must be said, our
happy, not predisposed to cajole
outside of town, our old enigmatic
not forked to lie or implore my kind
leaving I were to regret my foolhardy
from fall to flood to rapture to praising
beds trundled into our crypts, our wills
sweat-kilned bricks or local quarried
self-aggression, my naive wrestlings with
homage to everything, our rare bequeathals
they are, now that our very truths are hewn
beginning and far from my mortality, goading
reality or realistic fakery, my surprise insurance
the mode of maker or making, all gifts delivered
into self, this midday reckoning, won't soon pour
accidents or inevitabilities, our sense of ourselves
Suppose in some revelational by-and-by I give
beauty, infusing quality and satisfaction and
won't prevent conductivity or tranquil flow.
of thought and not mind or spirit or soul.
were to refuse my place, my love, my grace?

What we deem self-evident, what we believe stares at us from close range, what strikes us knowledge. If God were to someday meet me, if me there be, let the conversation be neither certainty, and it won't absolute. If I'm never to meet God, if God there never were, let imagination line breaks—let it rumble and blow and roil and strike—let it breathless itself across a landscape tend to my broken heart, if only for my span, my brief flicker out of darkness into darker darkness. be mended by silence. Suppose in some crop-circling I were to find myself a god, an unstraightened Fault me forever, if you must, this crack in time, my split vision, variate to distraction, my wish consign what I say to sideshow coughs, shouldn't condemn my song to trampled hay, straw-tough plunge, self-hurled into fascination, dead-weary of bliss, desiring to usher choice and mystery back plow the middle field. Suppose I were heroic and not ordinary, saintly and not common, allowed mud and dung of our human circus, neither a simpleton's fodder nor a scholar's grist, broken bales utter prayer, or just not the only prayer, what would be my reward? Suppose I were to speak plain, contemporary standards, the sleek thriving clique, torn by the wish to be wise and the need to be or impress but to nourish, or if not sustain, challenge, or if not seat, burn, the conflagrated carnival love of ornamentation set aside, our desire to accessorize curtailed, my tongue bent to its purpose, family or friends for approval, what would show as my fatal flaw? Suppose at the moment of my patterns of living, revel and destroy and repose, recover to ruin, our uncomfortable anglings Surprises haunt battlefields and playgrounds, parlors and attics, vales and shorelines alike, our to revolt, my fellow smiths enjoying inconsequential revolutions around the poem, my words as sleepwalks into white tornados, my stumblings into rash effort, my lonely experiments of God. Suppose creation weren't to praise creating—our active love, our imitation of good, our folded into our christenings, conception-shock to shroud-relief, now that we see things as granite, what would constitute my benediction? What if I were to word God out of my myself as injured opponent, wishing I had fought with pure confidence in either fake long-lasting and afforded, penetrating and wide, unconditional and singular, all in into our delicate codes, our pretty shifts, our permanent evolutions. This full funnel myself into animal awareness, consciousness a nifty trick developed over eons of bought with time, my victory as the understudy for my loss, what would be my plea? to grandchildren of posterity, every new gene honed into functionality and pragmatic understanding into my telling, into my told. This diasporic gash won't hamper exchange, as self-organizing and elegant, awkward and self-developed, my godlessness a condition myself sacrificial choice or favored status, what would I do if I were to reject my offer, if I substance into my song—what will become of us if our own imaginations aren't upheld?

IN ORDER OF APPEARANCE

Araboth

Nirvana

Happy Hunting Grounds

Jannah

The Way

Samsara

Paradise

Terra

Tian

Self

www.ingramcontent.com/pod-product-compliance
Lightning Source LLC
Chambersburg PA
CBHW042135060526
44119CB00117B/361